Essential

iPad

iOS 11 Edition

Kevin Wilson

Elluminet Press
www.elluminetpress.com

Essential iPad: iOS 11 Edition

Publisher: Elluminet Press
Director: Kevin Wilson
Lead Editor: Steven Ashmore
Technical Reviewer: Mike Taylor, Robert Ashcroft
Copy Editors: Joanne Taylor, James Marsh
Proof Reader: Mike Taylor
Indexer: James Marsh
Cover Designer: Kevin Wilson

eBook versions and licenses are also available for most titles. Any source code or other supplementary materials referenced by the author in this text is available to readers at

www.elluminetpress.com/resources

For detailed information about how to locate your book's source code, go to

www.elluminetpress.com/resources

Table of Contents

About the Author

Kevin Wilson has made a career out of technology and showing others how to use it. After earning a master's degree in computer science, software engineering, and multimedia systems, Kevin worked as a tutor and college instructor, helping students master such subjects as multimedia, computer literacy and information technology. He currently serves as Elluminet Press Publishing's senior writer and director, he periodically teaches computing at college in South Africa and serves as an IT trainer in England.

Kevin's motto is clear: "If you can't explain something simply, you haven't understood it well enough." To that end, he has created the Computer Essentials series, in which he breaks down complex technological subjects into smaller, easy-to-follow steps that students and ordinary computer users can put into practice.

Acknowledgements

Thanks to all the staff at Luminescent Media & Elluminet Press for their passion, dedication and hard work in the preparation and production of this book.

To all my friends and family for their continued support and encouragement in all my writing projects.

To all my colleagues, students and testers who took the time to test procedures and offer feedback on the book

Finally thanks to you the reader for choosing this book. I hope it helps you to use your iPad with greater ease.

Chapter 1

Setting up Your iPad

If you've just bought your new iPad and taken it out the box, the process to set it up to use for the first time is very simple. You don't even have to connect it to your computer.

With iOS 11, Apple have dropped support for the iPad 2, so iOS 11 can only be installed on the following devices.

iPad Pro models
iPad Air models
iPad 4th generation
iPad mini 4
iPad mini 3
iPad mini 2

iOS 11 is compatible with 64-bit devices only, so the iPhone 5, iPhone 5c, and iPad 2 do not support the software update.

So if you're upgrading your iPad, keep this in mind.

In this section we'll take a look at the processes of setting up your iPad when you turn it on for the first time.

Insert your SIM

Make sure your device is off before doing this. If your iPad has a SIM card or you're using an iPhone, you'll need to insert your SIM card from your network provider.

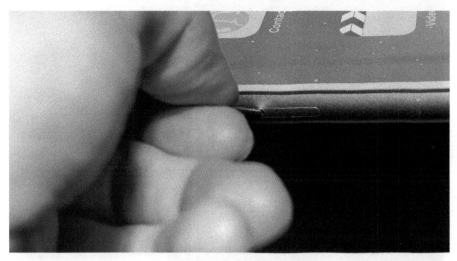

Push the end of a paper clip into the release hole on the side of your device. Pull out the little tray and insert your SIM.

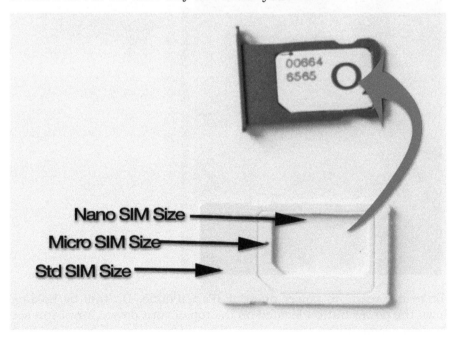

Nano SIM Size
Micro SIM Size
Std SIM Size

Chapter 1: Setting up Your iPad

Slide the little tray back into your device, until it fits firmly into place against the side.

You're not ready to power on your iPad/iPhone. Do this by holding down the power button located on the top of your device, until you see the Apple logo on the screen.

Power Up & Power Down

Once your iPad battery is fully charged, press and hold the power button for a couple of seconds until you see the apple logo.

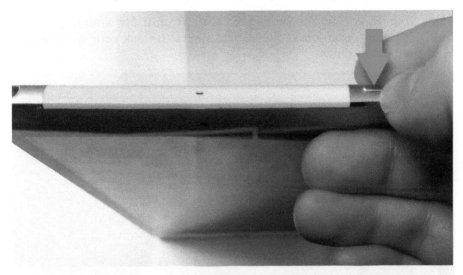

To completely shut down your iPad, press and hold the power button for a few seconds, until you see the shut down slider on your screen. Slide your finger across the slider to shut down your iPad.

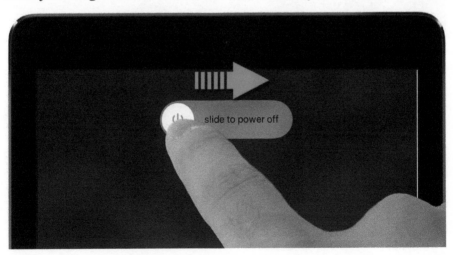

It's a good a idea to completely power down your iPad from time to time to reset its resources - this can help when your iPad seems to be running slower than usual. Most of the time your iPad goes into sleep mode when in normal use.

Unlock & Wake iPad

The home button also contains a finger print scanner and is usually set up during the initial setup.

Place your finger on the button so your thumb fits snugly into the button's indent, then press the button once to unlock your iPad - **don't** hold the button down.

If you haven't set up your finger print scanner, you'll be prompted for your passcode. This is the code you enter during the initial setup procedure.

Force Shutdown

Sometimes your iPad can become unresponsive or freeze. When this happens you can force a shutdown.

To do this, hold down the power button on the top, and the home button at the same time until the screen goes blank.

Once the screen has gone blank, wait a few seconds, then press and hold the power button for a couple of seconds, until the apple logo appears on screen.

Upgrading your iPad to iOS 11

Make sure your iPad is plugged into a power charger and that it is connected to your WiFi.

Once you have done that, go to the settings app and tap 'General' then 'Software Update'.

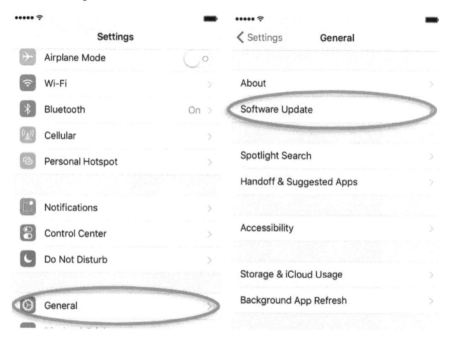

Tap Download and Install.

To update now, tap Install. Enter your passcode when prompted. Your iPad will restart and the update will start. This might take a while. Once it has finished, you'll need to go through the initial setup.

Initial Setup

To use iPad, you need and internet connection and an Apple ID for some features.

Turn iPad on and follow the Setup Assistant. This will guide you through the process

Swipe your finger across the bottom of the screen.

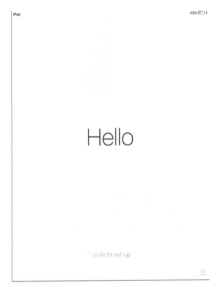

Select Language, scroll down and Select Country or Region.

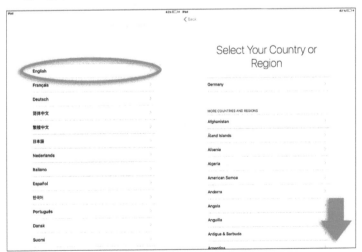

Chapter 1: Setting up Your iPad

Tap on the name of your Wi-Fi Network. Enter your wifi password or network key when prompted.

Tap 'Enable Location Services'. The location services allow your iPad to determine your current physical location. Some apps require this; maps and other apps that provide local information.

Enter a passcode and set up touch ID if you have it. This is used to lock your iPad and you will be prompted for this code when you slide open your iPad from the lock screen.

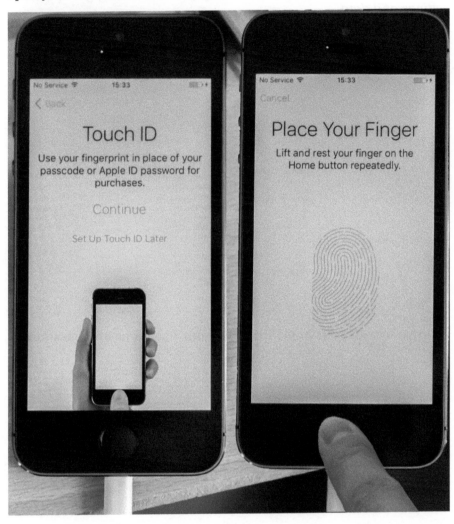

For touch ID, scan the finger you are most likely to use to press the home button with. In most cases this is your thumb, so it makes sense to scan this finger.

You'll need to scan your finger a few times, so the system can account for different variables as you wont always put your thumb on the pad in exactly the same position every time.

Your device will tell you when it's done. Tap next.

Chapter 1: Setting up Your iPad

Tap 'set up as New iPad'. This will create a clean iPad. *If you have upgraded to a new iPad, you can tap 'restore from iCloud backup' and select the latest backup. This will set up your iPad using your previous settings and data.*

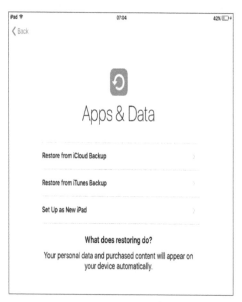

Tap sign in with your Apple ID. Enter your username and password.

Set up iCloud Keychain. Keychain keeps your usernames, passwords, and credit card numbers stored behind 256-bit encryption on Apple's iCloud servers, to save you the hassle of typing them in every time you need them.

Apple Diagnostics. Tap 'don't send'.

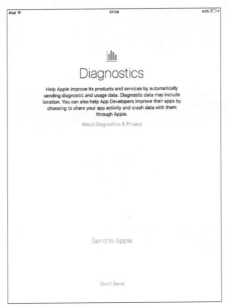

Tap OK to Get Started.

Chapter 1: Setting up Your iPad

When you sign into your iPad you will see the home screen. Lets take a closer look at the screen.

Along the top of the home screen there is a status bar that displays current networks (cellular or wifi), current time, services such as bluetooth and battery life.

In the centre of the screen are icons representing apps that are currently installed on iPad. Some are installed already but many can be downloaded from the app store.

Along the bottom of the screen is the Dock. The Dock is split into two sections. On the left hand side you'll see your most used apps: messages, web browsing, email, music, and files. You can drag and drop icons onto this part of the dock from your home screen. On the right hand side of the dock, you'll see your most recently opened apps.

At the bottom of the iPad itself, we have the home button. Whenever you want to get back to the home screen from any app, just press this button.

This diagram shows the rear. You can see volume controls and SIM card tray on the left of the diagram. On the back you'll see your camera, the headphone jack along the top and the dock connector along the bottom.

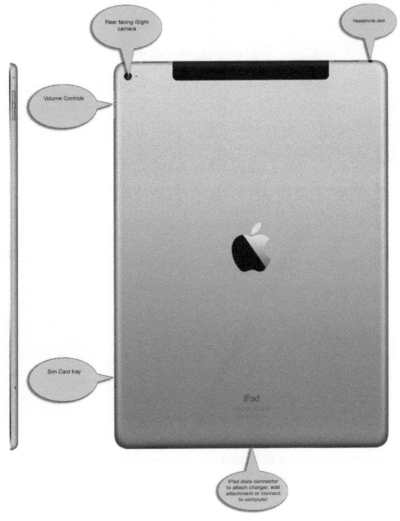

Charging your iPad's Battery

You can plug your iPad directly into the charger to charge the battery, without having to go through a computer.

Plug the other end of the lightning cable into the port on the bottom of your iPad.

Your battery will take a few hours to charge. Best practice is not to let your battery deplete completely, charge it up when you still have about 20% charge left.

Connecting your iPad to a Mac/PC

Your iPad lightning cable connects to the port on the bottom of your iPad.

The other end of the cable can be plugged into a PC or Mac to allow you to load on music, photos, apps etc.

Using iTunes

To access your iPad from a computer you will need to have iTunes installed on your computer. If you are using a Mac, iTunes will already be installed. If you are on a PC then you need to download the software from Apple's website.

You can download it from

`www.apple.com/itunes`

On iTunes' website, click the download link on the top right.

Then on the next page remove the ticks from the two boxes shown below.

Download iTunes

X   iTunes 11.3.1 for Mac OS X

☑ Send me iTunes updates, news, and special offers.

☑ Keep me up to date with Apple news, software updates, and the latest information on products and services.

Apple Customer Privacy Policy

Email Address

Location
⦿ United Kingdom
◯ Other

Why do we need this?

Download Now ↓

If you want apple to send you lots of notifications via email, enter email address. Otherwise leave it blank.

Click the 'download now' button. Go to your downloads folder and double click the iTunes installer. It is usually called 'iTunes6464Setup'

26

Once iTunes has installed, sign in with your Apple ID and password.

Syncing your iPad with your Mac/PC

Plug your iPad into your computer, iTunes will take a few moments to recognise your device.

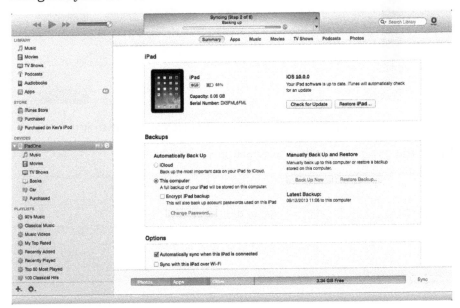

Connecting to the Internet

With an iPad, you can connect to the internet two ways: one is using WiFi and the other is using a cellular connection if you've inserted a SIM card. In this section, we'll take a look at connecting using WiFi

Wi-Fi

Wi-Fi is often faster than cellular data networks, but may not be available in many locations.

To locate nearby Wi-Fi networks, tap Settings on your home screen.

Tap Wi-Fi, then tap the name of the network you want to join

Enter the wifi password or network key.

Once you have done that tap Join.

For your home WiFi, the network key or password is usually printed on the back of your router.

Sometimes the network name is called an SSID.

Use the same procedure if you are on a public hotspot such as in a cafe, library, hotel, airport and so on. You'll need to find the network key if they have one. Some are open networks and you can just connect.

When using public hotspots, keep in mind that most of them don't encrypt the data you send over the internet and aren't secure. So don't start checking your online banking account or shop online while using an unsecured connection, as anyone who is on the public wifi hotspot can potentially gain access to anything you do.

If you're really concerned about security or use your devices on public hotspots for work, then you should consider a VPN or Virtual Private Network. A VPN encrypts all the data you send and receive over a network. There are a few good ones to choose from, some have a free option with a limited amount of data and others you pay a subscription.

Take a look at www.tunnelbear.com, windscribe.com & speedify.com

Setting up Email Accounts

Tap the settings app icon on your home screen

Scroll down to 'accounts & passwords'.

On the right hand side at the top, tap 'add account'.

Tap the type of account you want to add. This can be a Hotmail, Gmail, iCloud, Yahoo or a Microsoft Account.

In this example I am going to add a Microsoft Account. So tap on 'outlook.com'

In the box that appears, enter your account email address, tap 'next', then your password.

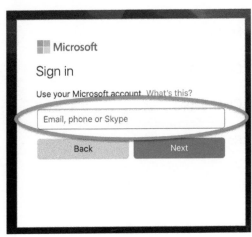

Tap 'next'.

Chapter 1: Setting up Your iPad

Select 'yes' to the permission confirmation, to allow your iPad to access your email account.

iOS needs you to confirm its permission to:

- **Sync your emails, contacts, calendar and tasks, and send emails**
- **Access your info at any time**
- **Sign you in**
- **View your basic profile**

You can change these application permissions at any time in your account settings.

Yes   No

Select what you want your iPad to sync from the mail server. You can copy email, contacts, your calendar and any reminders onto your iPad by turning all the toggle switches to green, as shown below.

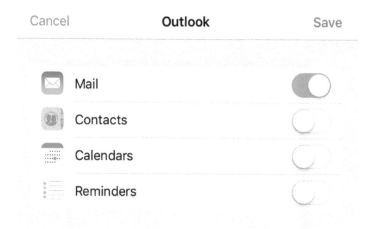

Tap 'Save'.

Use the same procedure for any other email accounts you may have; yahoo or gmail.

Add Social Media Accounts

You can add your Facebook and Twitter accounts to your iPad. The easiest way to do this is to go to the App Store and download the app for Facebook and the app for Twitter.

Tap on the App Store icon on your home screen and in the search field on the top right type 'facebook'.

Tap 'get', next to the Facebook icon to download it. This icon might also look like a cloud, if you have downloaded it before, on another device such as an iPod or iPhone.

Once it has download, hit your home button, then tap the Facebook icon on your home screen.

You can now sign in with your Facebook username and password.

You can use the same procedure to setup Twitter, Instagram and any other social media account you have.

Change your Wallpaper

You can set a photograph as a background on your lock screen and home screen.

You can do this from inside the Photos App. Tap the photograph you want to set.

Tap the share icon on the top right of the screen. This will open up some sharing options along the bottom.

From the options that appear, select 'use as wallpaper'.

Drag the photograph with your finger until it's in the desired position. You can also make the photograph smaller, by pinching the screen with your thumb and forefinger.

To set as both home and lock screen tap 'set both'. If you just want the photo on your home screen, tap 'set home screen'. Likewise for lock screen.

Getting Around Your iPad

Chapter 2

The iPad runs Apple's own operating system called iOS10 and is easy to learn and use. There are a large selection of third-party apps available from the App Store, in categories from productivity to entertainment.

In this section we will look at some of the built in apps and the most commonly used apps from the app store.

Lets begin by having a look at some of the iPad models on the market and a few of the new features of iPad.

iPads on Offer

There are currently three models available. The iPad Mini, the iPad Air and the iPad Pro.

Without getting too technical, these models are more or less identical, with a few exceptions worth noting.

iPad Pro

- 12.9" or 9.7" inch screen, fast CPU, with 32GB - 256GB memory
- Nano-SIM (supports Apple SIM), 4 speaker
- You can even attach external keyboards, useful if you use your iPad to do your work.

iPad Air

- 9.7" inch screen, with 16GB - 64GB memory
- Nano-SIM (supports Apple SIM), 2 speaker

iPad Mini

- 7.9" inch screen, with 16GB - 128GB memory
- Nano-SIM (supports Apple SIM), 2 speaker

These features can change at any time, so for a more up to date comparison and pricing, go here www.apple.com/ipad/compare/

Sign in & Sign Out of iCloud

If you've set up your iPad from new and been through the initial setup, then your iPad will normally be signed in to your iCloud account. However if you need to sign into another iPad then you can do so from the settings.

To sign in, open your settings app, tap on 'sign in to your iPad' and enter your apple id email address and password.

To sign out, open your settings app, tap on your apple id, then on the bottom right hand side, tap 'sign out'.

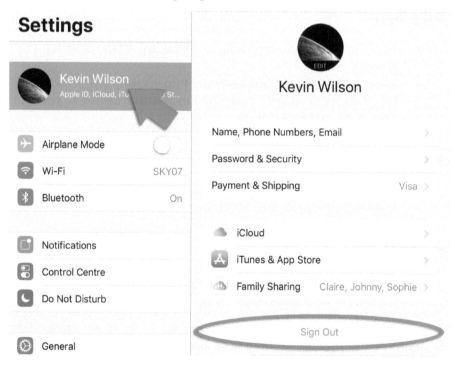

Apple ID

phwwright@yahoo.co.uk

Password

Apple*030* cpu* 2015* 32*

Ipad   Passcode

4414

41929-1695-3293-6019

BBC   B/W

13 Oct 1932

Facebook ?

030 cpv Fbk

Touch Gestures

Gestures, sometimes called multi-touch gestures, are what you'll use to interact with the touch screen on iPad.

All it takes is the touch of a finger to use your favourite apps, navigate the web, and access all the things you need.

Tap

Tap your index finger on an icon or select something on the screen.

For example, you can tap on an app icon, a link in safari or even a song you want to download.

You can also tap and hold your finger on the screen to access other options that might be available (this is like right-clicking the mouse on your computer).

Drag

Tap on the screen and without lifting your finger off run your finger across to drag up and down, left or right, or any other direction on the screen.

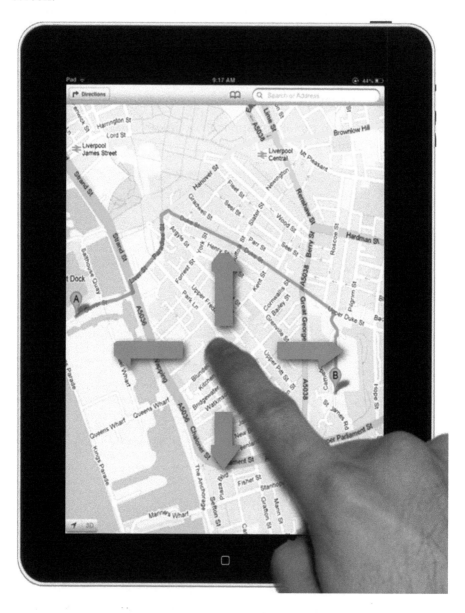

Pinch & Spread

Hold your index finger and thumb on the area you want to zoom in or out on and pinch the screen to zoom in and spread to zoom out.

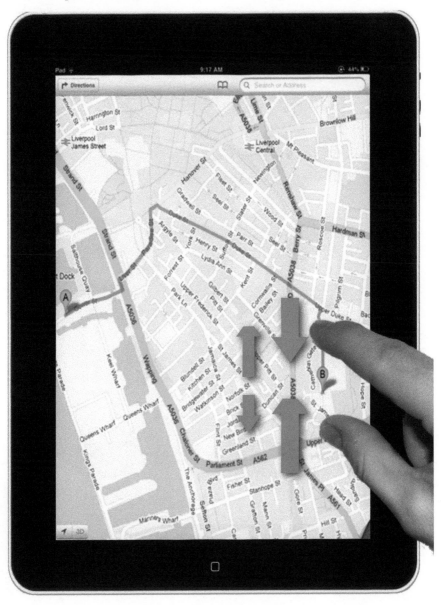

Pinch is shown in the illustration above, with the large red arrow, spread is shown with the small red arrow.

Swipe

This allows you to flip through photos, pages in an e-book, pages on the home screen. You swipe almost like striking a match.

Four Finger Swipe

Hold your four fingers (not your thumb) on the screen and swipe across to switch between open apps.

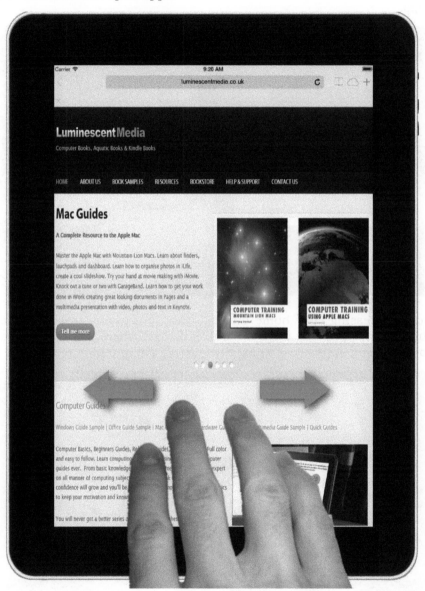

Home Button

While using your iPad, pressing the home button once will bring you back to your home screen, where you can select your icons to launch apps.

Double pressing your home button - that is pressing twice in quick succession, will bring up your control centre, where you can view all your running apps, close apps, turn on/off wifi and blue tooth.

3D Touch

The latest screens on iPads and iPhones are now pressure sensitive, so your iPad can tell how hard you press. 3D Touch detects how hard you press on your iPad's screen.

We're all used to tapping on icons to start different apps or to select options and so on. 3D touch adds a new method called a press. To press on an icon means to push it, applying a bit of pressure, as if you are pressing a button.

You can now press on the icons on your home screen to quickly access some basic features, without opening the app. For example, to take a quick selfie, press on the camera icon, and from the drop down, tap 'take selfie'.

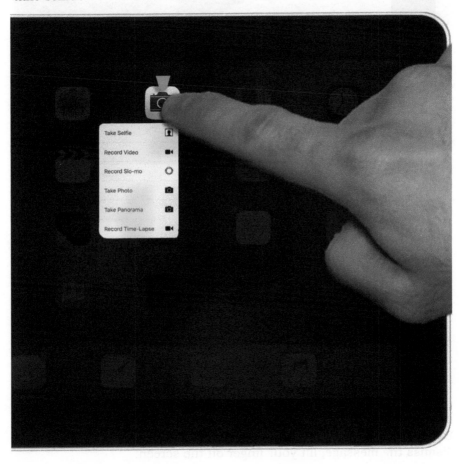

You can do this with any app on the home screen. These are called quick actions.

Another feature is called 'peek and pop'. If you are, for example, checking through your emails, you can press and hold on a message in your inbox to quickly preview the message.

A quick preview will open up. This is called 'peek'. From here, you can swipe up with your finger to reply without opening the email.

To open the email fully, press down again. This is called 'pop'. To dismiss the message, lift your finger off the screen.

You can use these features, on maps, photos, messages and so on. Give it a try and see what it does.

Quick Peek Home Screen Icons

If you tap and hold your finger on an icon either on the dock or home screen for about a second, you'll see the peek window appear. This shows you the last few items you were looking at or working on within that particular app.

For example, in the screen below, tap and hold your finger on the pages app icon - either on the dock or on the home screen.

Multitasking

iOS is called a multitasking operating system. This means that you can run more than one app at a time. Most apps will be running in the background. To quickly see what apps are running, press your home button twice.

After using your iPad, you will find that there are a lot of apps running, this can severely affect the performance of your iPad and drain your battery more quickly.

To close apps, press your home button twice, then swipe your finger upwards on the app you want to close, as illustrated below.

This will close the app. Do this on all the apps you want to close.

You can also use this technique to switch between apps. Press your home button twice, then swipe your finger left and right to browse through the apps, then tap on the app you want to switch to.

Open Multiple Apps at a Time

You can open multiple apps using two new methods. You can use slide over, where your app floats on top of the other and split view, where your apps run side by side..

Using Slide Over

While running an app, swipe upwards from the bottom edge of the screen to reveal the dock, then drag an app icon up into your screen

Your app will open up and float on top of your screen.

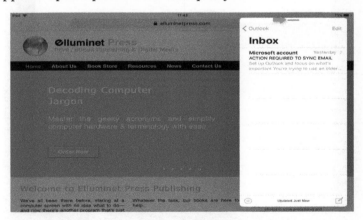

You can interact with your app in the normal way and you can drag the app to either side of the screen. Use the small tab on top of the window to drag.

Using Split View

While running an app, swipe upwards from the bottom edge of the screen to reveal the dock, then drag an app icon up into your workspace

Now, find the small tab on the top of the window. Tap and swipe your finger upwards on the tab.

Your screen will split and you'll see one app on the left hand side and the app you just opened on the right.

You can drag and drop information between the apps, as well as copy and paste information.

Drag & Drop

The Drag and Drop feature allows you to drag text, photos or documents from one app to another. You can drag items within the same apps or across different apps

In the demo below, the email app is running with files app running as a slide over app, as demonstrated in the previous section.

Tap and hold your finger on an item - photo or file, then drag your finger across the screen and drop the item where you want.

You can also drag and drop using the split view. Open the two apps in split view as demonstrated in the previous section.

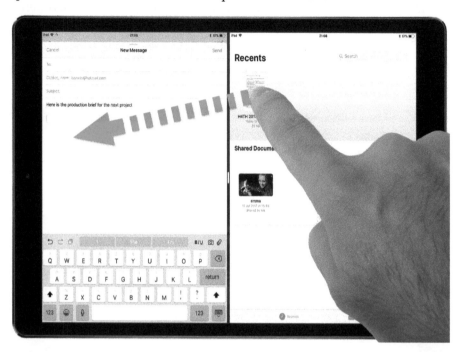

In the demonstration above, I have the email app running in split view with the files app.

To attach the document to the email, tap and hold your finger on the document in the files app, and drag it across to the email app.

Control Centre

The control centre, also sometimes called the command centre, is your control hub where you can adjust screen brightness, volume, access wifi/bluetooth controls, access your camera and see your currently running apps.

To open control centre, swipe your finger upwards from the bottom edge of the screen, or double press the home button on the bottom of your iPad. If you're opening control centre from an app rather than your home screen, you'll need to swipe upwards from the bottom edge of your screen once to reveal the dock, then swipe upwards again to reveal control centre.

Here you can control the volume of playing music, turn on and off wifi, blue-tooth, access your camera, set the orientation lock to stop the screen shifting - this can be useful if you are reading a book etc.

Customising Control Centre

To customise the controls, first open your settings app. Tap 'Control Centre' then tap 'Customise Controls'.

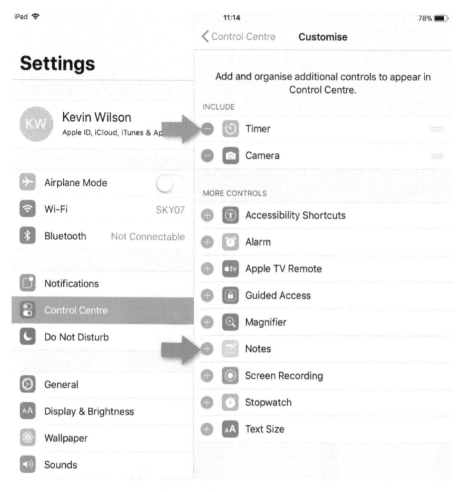

The settings for this are divided into two sections. The top section labelled 'include', shows apps and icons that will appear in the control centre. The bottom section labelled 'more controls', shows apps and features that are available but are not enabled.

To remove apps or icons from control centre, tap the red '-' next to the app name in the top section.

To add apps or icons, tap the green '+'next to the app in the bottom section. The enabled app or icon will jump to the top section, meaning it is now enabled and will show up on the control centre.

Notifications & Lock Screen

These two have now been merged. Swipe your finger downwards from the top edge of the screen, will invoke the lock screen.

Notifications such as email, sms/text messages or reminders can also appear on the lock screen.

Tap on one of the notifications to see more information.

Picture in Picture

Picture in Picture is for video. This can be FaceTime video or a film from your video library. The video shows up as a small thumbnail that can sit over the other apps you're using.

Tap the little icon on the top left of the video window while watching a video on your video player, the video will turn into a thumbnail.

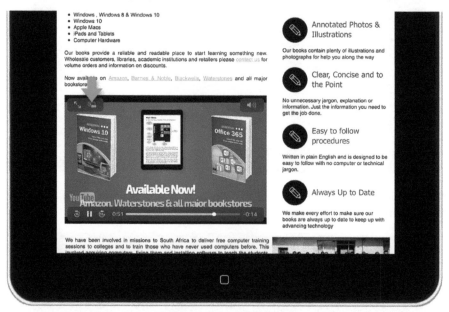

You can also drag the thumbnail into position. You can now go back to the home screen, open another app and the video will remain on top so you can see it while working on something else.

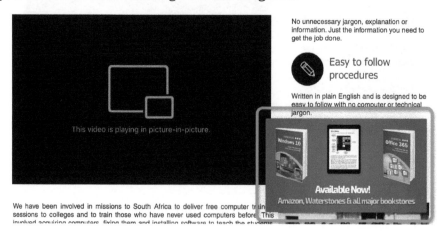

If you now go back to your home screen, the video stays in the corner

You can open any app and continue working. In this example, I am going to open the email app.

Continuity

Continuity allows users to share documents, e-mails, and websites over Wi-Fi to your devices.

For example, when you're working on an email, Pages document, Keynote presentation, Numbers spreadsheet, viewing a location in Maps or if you're browsing the web on your Mac, you will see on the lock screen of your iPad, the app you're currently using on your Mac.

Your iPad will allow you to pick up where you left off in that app you were using on your Mac. This is called handoff.

Tap the small icon on the bottom left of the lock screen, then swipe your finger upwards.

Continuity also allows you to reply to SMS messages and answer phone calls on you Mac and iPad. This feature is supported only by compatible Macs running OS X Yosemite, Capitan and Sierra, or by devices running iOS 8, 9, 10 & 11.

The On-screen Keyboard

Typing on an iPad is easy, using the on-screen Multi-Touch keyboard. Tap in any text field, email, document or message, and the on screen keyboard will pop up on the bottom of the screen.

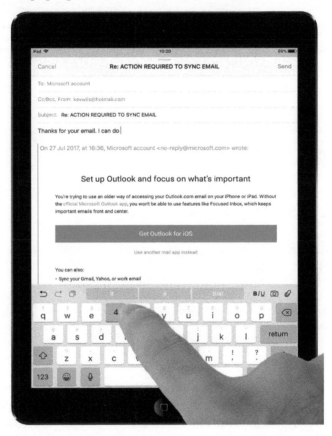

You can tap on the keys to type. To access the numbers and symbols on the top half of the key, tap and slide your finger down on the key. This is like holding down the shift key on a computer. For example, to type 4, tap and slide your finger down on the letter R.

Lets take a closer look at the keyboard. You'll notice some icons and information along the top of they keyboard. Some of these will depend on which app you are typing in but most have a similar function.

Here is an example from the email app.

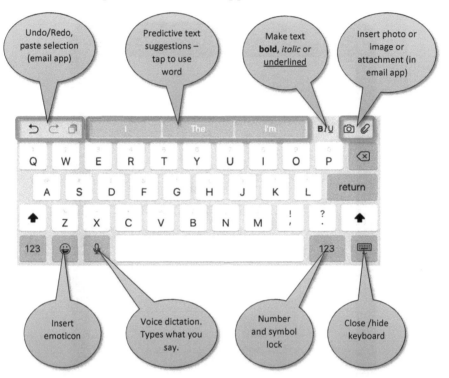

Along the top you will see some predictive text suggestions that appear according to what you're typing in. If the correct word appears, you can quickly tap on the appropriate suggestion instead of typing in the whole word.

On either side of the predictive text section, you'll see some app specific icons. These are usually shortcuts to common tools used in these apps. For example inserting photos or attachments in our email example or changing text to bold or italic.

Some icons along the bottom worth noting are: the '123' key, this locks in numbers and symbols so you can quickly enter a series of numbers just by tapping the keys. The 'smiley face' icon, these are emojis or emoticons - small smiley faces, thumbs up, expressions, and small images that are intended to show how you're feeling in your messages; happy, angry, amused and so on. Finally the 'microphone icon', this is a dictation tool that transcribes or types out voice dictations.

External Keyboard

Only really available on the iPad pro, however there are third party bluetooth keyboards that will work to some extent.

On the iPad pro, the iPad keyboard slots into a special connector on the side. Other iPads don't have this and you'll need to use a bluetooth keyboard similar to the ones pictured below.

You can pick them up online or any computer store.

Apple Pencil

Only really available on the iPad pro, but has some limited use on other iPads too such as doodling and handwritten notes.

You'll need to purchase an Apple Pencil to use this feature and at the time of writing, they are quite expensive.

Use your pencil on Microsoft Word, Excel and PowerPoint; add annotations and handwritten notes.

There are also some artistic apps where you can apply pressure to create darker lines or tilt your pencil to shade in areas.

Just type 'apple pencil' into the search field in the app store and you'll find plenty of apps.

Spotlight Search

Spotlight is integrated with a number of web services so that users can search using Wikipedia, Bing, or Google. Other services include: news, nearby places, suggested websites, movie show times, and content that is not already on the device from the iTunes Store

You can activate spotlight search by swiping your finger downwards from the centre of your home screen.

Once you have spotlight's search screen, you can type your search into the search field at the top of the screen.

Search also gives you some suggestions. These are listed below the search field and are the most commonly searched for entries for your search term. In the example below, I am searching for anything relating to 'computer'. Tap on the entry that best matches your search, or press enter on your on screen keyboard.

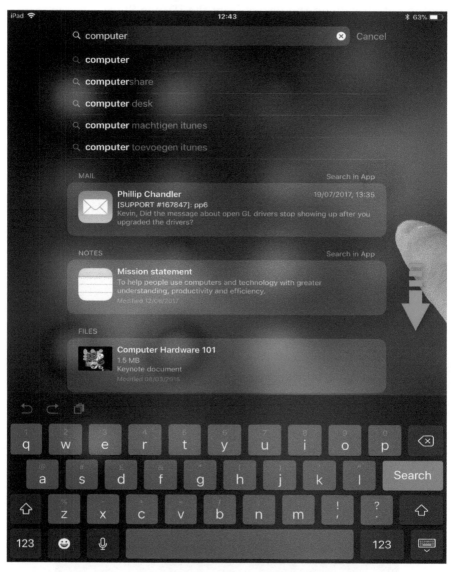

Scroll down the list to see files, apps, websites, news articles, and suggested websites according to your search terms.

Tap on one of the items to open it up.

You can track flights. This is a useful feature, especially if you have arranged to pick up a friend or collect a colleague from the airport.

If you have the flight number, enter it into spotlight search. There might be more than one flight, so make sure you confirm the correct departure and arrival times.

Tap on the flight to view tracking details. Here you'll see the current position of the aircraft on the map, which terminal the plane is arriving at and what time it is arriving - this plane is arriving at terminal 3 at 14:45.

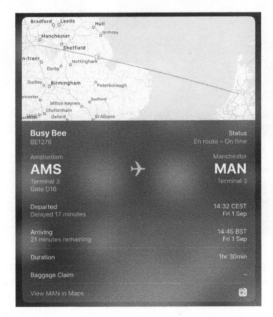

Underneath you'll also see baggage claim timings and how long passengers are expected to get through. At the bottom you can find driving directions to the airport using the maps app.

Arranging Icons

On your home screen tap and hold your finger on one of the icons.

A little x will appear on the top left of the icon. This means you can move icons around the screen or onto the next page. To move an icon tap and hold your finger on an icon, then move your finger to drag the icon.

For icons you use the most, you can drag them to your dock at the bottom.

You can get to the other pages by swiping your finger left and right to turn the page

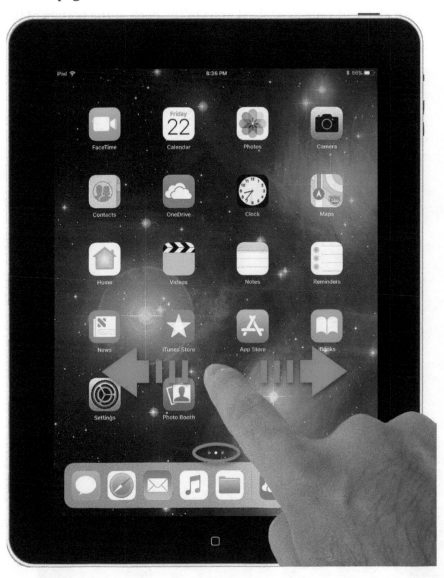

The two little dots, circled in the illustration above, show you what page you are on and how many pages of icons you have. This will vary depending on what apps you have installed. In this example, there are two pages.

You can identify what page you are on by looking at this icon, the one in bold is the page you are on. In this example, page 1.

Adding Icons to the Dock

You can also add your most used apps to the dock at the bottom of the screen. To do this, tap, and hold your finger on an icon until it starts to wobble.

Drag the icon with your finger to the dock.

Siri

Siri is an extremely useful feature. She allows you to talk to your iPad, sometimes referred to as a virtual assistant; she can help you with all kinds of things. You can use Siri to send messages, schedule meetings, and search for nearby restaurants all without having to type a single letter.

Using Siri

To use Siri, press and hold the Home button on your device until she appears. Then tell her what you need.

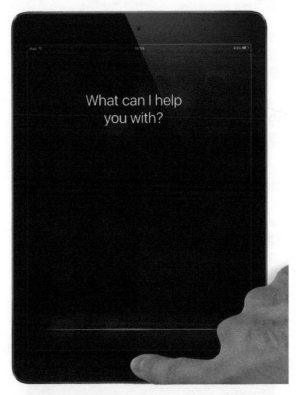

Try some of the following phrases...

Try saying: "Hey Siri"
Try saying: "Send email to..." (pick a name from your contacts list)
Try saying: "What is the weather like tomorrow"
Try saying: "Find me a website on baking a cake"
Try saying: "Remind me to pick up milk on the way home"
Try saying: "Call..." (pick a name from your contacts list).

Siri Translate

Here's a good one for those who love to travel but don't speak the local language. At the time of writing, Siri can only translate from US English to French, German, Italian, Mandarin and Spanish.

If you're using Siri with any language other than US English, you'll need to change this in the settings app. Tap 'Siri & Search', tap to change the language to 'English (United States)', circled below.

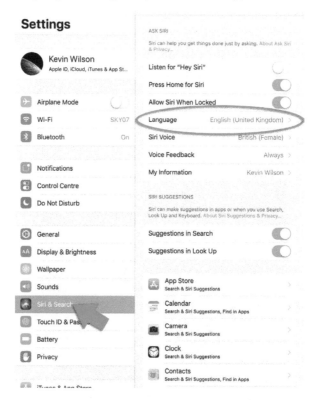

To use the translator, hold down the home button until Siri appears and speak the word **"Translate"**.

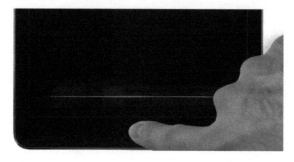

Siri will ask you which language you want to translate into. Say the language name or tap the option from the list. In this demonstration, I'm going to use Spanish.

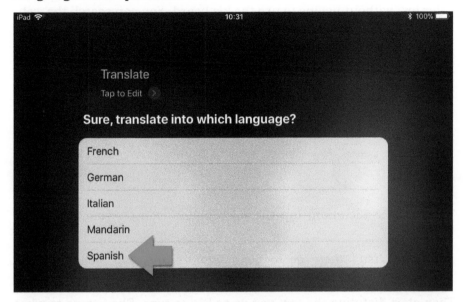

Now speak the phrase you want to translate into the language you just selected.

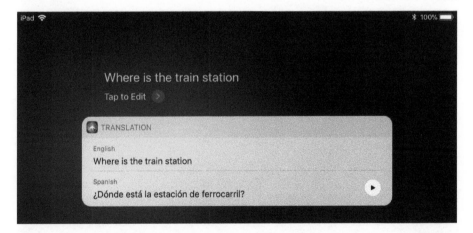

To play the translation again, tap the play button next to the translation.

You can also say "How do I say <u>where is the train station</u> in <u>spanish</u>?"

Just replace the underlined bits of the phrase for the phrase and language you want to translate into.

Voice Dictation

Another useful feature of Siri is voice dictation, which allows you to enter text without having to use the keyboard. You can search the web, take notes, post an update to Facebook, and more just by speaking.

To use voice dictation, tap the microphone icon on your on screen keyboard.

If the icon isn't there go to your settings app, tap 'general', then 'keyboard'. Go down to 'enable dictation' and switch the slider to on.

Then start dictating the text you want Siri to type. She listens to what you say, and types it. The more you use it, the better Siri gets at understanding you.

You can even add punctuation by saying words like "period" or 2 "question mark" when you reach the end of a sentence. Tap the keyboard icon on the bottom right to close dictation mode.

Settings Search

Tap on the settings app. On the main screen at the top left, swipe your finger down under the word 'settings'

This will reveal the settings search field.

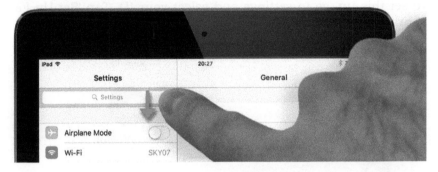

In the search field, type in the setting you want to change. I'm adding my email accounts so I'll type 'mail' in this example.

Tap on 'mail' in the search results.

Family Sharing

You can now add six others users as family members. You can share iTunes and Apps, Apple Music, iCloud Storage, your location and authorize your kid's spending on the app store.

To set this up, go to settings and select your ID. Tap 'Set Up Family Sharing'. Then tap 'get started'.

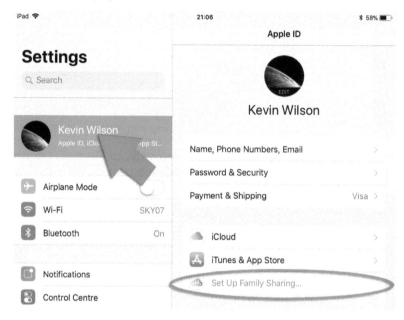

You'll see a screen with four options. You can share any of these options later on but this screen is asking which one you want to begin with. If you want to share books, apps, films and music; select the first option.

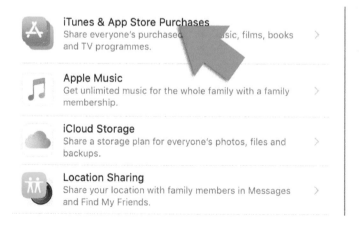

Tap 'continue' to confirm you want to use your Apple ID to share your purchases.

Confirm the payment details you want to share. Any member of your family that requests an app will be charged to this payment method on your approval. If you want to use another one tap 'use different payment method' and enter the card details.

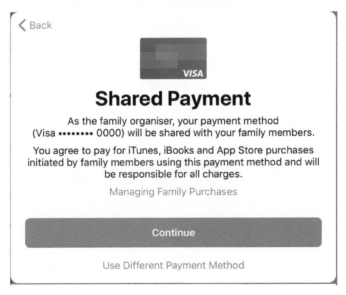

Tap 'continue' if you want to use your default apple id payment method.

Tap 'invite family members'. Select 'invite in person' and enter their apple id email address. If they don't have an email address or too young, tap 'create a child account'.

Add a Family Member

Go to settings, select your ID. Tap 'family sharing then tap 'add family member'.

Now select how you want to invite them. You can invite then 'in person', ie enter their apple id email address, send an invitation via iMessage or 'create a new child account'.

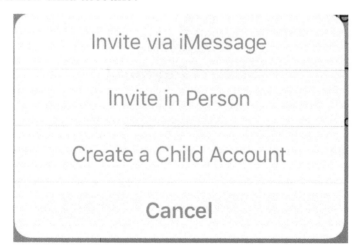

Invite in Person

Select 'invite in person' from the popup. Enter the person's apple id email address and password. If their details are in your address book, you'll see a suggestion underneath. Tap on the name if it's correct.

When the person signs into their iPad and checks their email, they'll see an invitation to join the family.

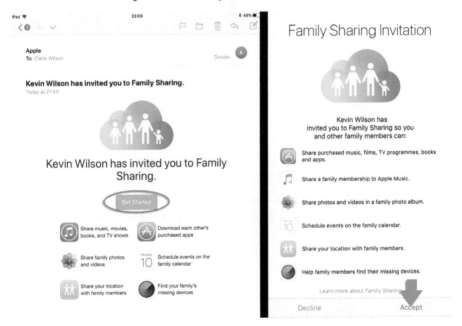

Click 'get started', then click 'accept' on the confirmation.

Child Accounts

If you have young children it makes sense to create separate accounts for them rather than allowing them to use yours. This helps to protect them and to help you monitor what your child is up to.

To create a child account, go to settings, select your ID. Tap 'family sharing' then tap 'add family member'. From the popup select 'create child account'.

Now follow the instructions on screen. Tap 'next' to get to the next screen.

Enter your child's birthday. When you tap 'next' you may be prompted to enter your CVV code from the credit card you have registered with your apple id.

Enter it and tap 'next'.

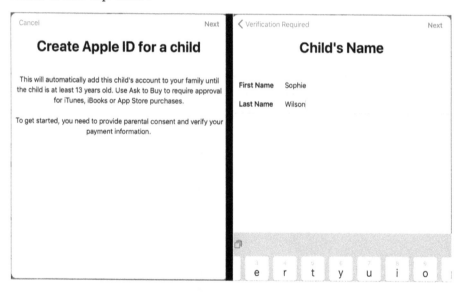

Enter your child's name and enter an apple id email and password for them. This will create a new account for your child to use.

Now, select some security questions that you will remember the answers to. This is a security step that will be used to identify you when you need to change a password or recover a forgotten password.

Select a question from the 'question' field and type in an answer in the 'answer' field. Tap 'agree' to accept the terms and conditions

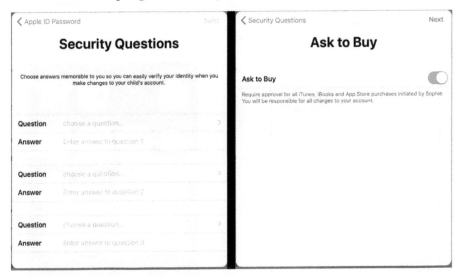

Enable 'ask to buy'. This means that if your child tries to buy an app from the app store, a music track, tv show or film, you will receive an authorisation request where you can approve the purchase or deny it.

Now allow your child to sign into their iPad with the apple id email address and password you just created. In this example it would be sophie20077@icloud.com

Managing your Family

Family members can share purchased apps, music, and books using the same credit card. iPad can also automatically set up photo streams for all family members. Calendars may be synced between all members.

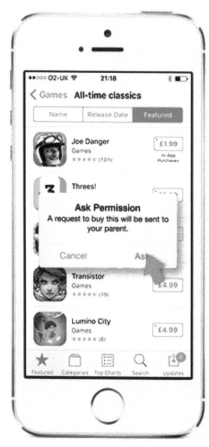 

Kids can also send iTunes and App Store download requests for apps, music, movies, and more to their parents provided this service is set up correctly.

On your device, tap 'review' from the prompt to see details of the request.

Chapter 3

Internet, Email, Communication

Your iPad has a lot of features that allow you to connect to the internet, browse the web, send and receive emails, share pictures with friends, store addresses and contacts, have video chat conversations with family.

To do this, Apple have provided some built in apps; Safari for web browsing, Mail for email and Face Time for video chat.

You also have Apps for social media, and an address book to keep track of contacts addresses and details.

Lets start by taking a look at Safari web browser.

Using Safari

To launch safari, tap on the safari icon located on your dock.

This will launch safari's and you'll see the main screen. Here is a summary of what the icons do.

In safari's main screen, tap in the website address field, to enter the website's address, or google search keyword.

Two menus to take note of. The first menu is on the left hand side of the screen and allows you to access favourite or bookmarked sites. You can tap on any of these in the list to return to the sites.

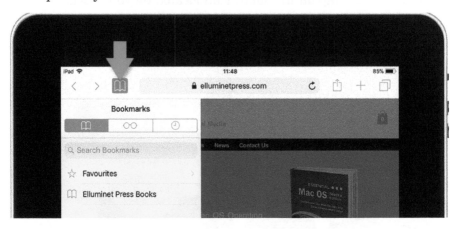

The second, is on the right hand side and allows you to share the current website link via text message, email or social media. Just tap on the icon to share the site on twitter or facebook, email the link or send it via text.

Along the bottom of that menu, you can add the current site to bookmarks/favourites. To do this tap bookmark.

Hit the + sign to add a new tab where you can open another website, google search, favourite and so on.

The final icon on the right hand side, allows you to see all the tabs you currently have open

Safari will display your open tabs/websites as thumbnail previews, you can tap on to open up.

Reader View

Reader view makes it easier to read web pages without all the unnecessary background clutter that usually comes with a website.

Reader view is not available on all web pages but is on most. To enable reader view, tap the reader icon on the left hand side of the web address search field.

Here you can see on the left, the normal view and on the right you can see the reader view.

The reader view is designed to improve readability on screen and often removes a lot of graphics, photos and other media, so it's worth keeping this in mind if you are visiting media rich websites.

Tap the same icon to go back to normal view.

Using Email

To start the mail app, tap Mail on the bottom of the screen.

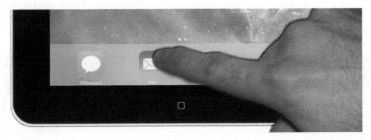

Once your email is setup it will open on the main screen. The email app works best if you use your iPad in horizontal orientation. On the left hand side, is a list of all your emails. Just tap on one to view.

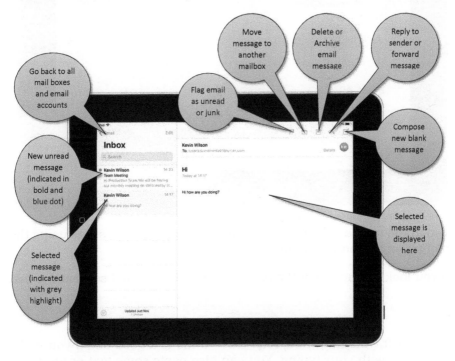

To reply to an email, select the email you want from your inbox, then tap the 'reply to sender' icon on the top right.

To forward or print an email, tap and hold your finger on the 'reply to sender' icon and select 'forward' to forward the email to someone else, tap 'print' to print the email.

To send a new message, click the 'compose new email' icon on the top right. This will bring up a new email. Tap in the 'To:' field to enter an email address. If you are replying to a message, the email address of the person that sent you the message will appear here automatically.

Tap in the subject field and add some text.

Tap in the message body underneath and type your message using the pop up on screen keyboard.

If you look on the top of the on screen keyboard you'll see some icons.

On the left, you can undo/redo text - undo is a good one if you make a mistake with your typing. You can also paste some text or an image you have copied from somewhere else. In the centre you have some text predictions - this shows up words you're most likely to type while writing your email - tap word to insert into message. Over on the right, you can change your text to bold, italic or underlined. You can insert a photo directly from your camera, and add an attachment.

When you have finished, tap send.

To save time, if you have 3D touch enabled, you can press and hold on a message in your inbox to quickly preview the message.

A quick preview will open up. This is called 'peek'. From here, you can swipe up with your finger to reply without opening the email.

To open the email fully, press down again. This is called 'pop'. To dismiss the message, lift your finger off.

Contacts

The Contacts App is your address book. It contains all the names, email addresses, phone numbers and addresses of the people you correspond with.

Launch address book by tapping on the icon on your home screen.

This is the main screen. You can browse contacts, or add new ones.

Tap on the + sign to add a new contact.

On the screen that appears, enter their name and contact details in the fields.

Add their phone number, and email addresses.

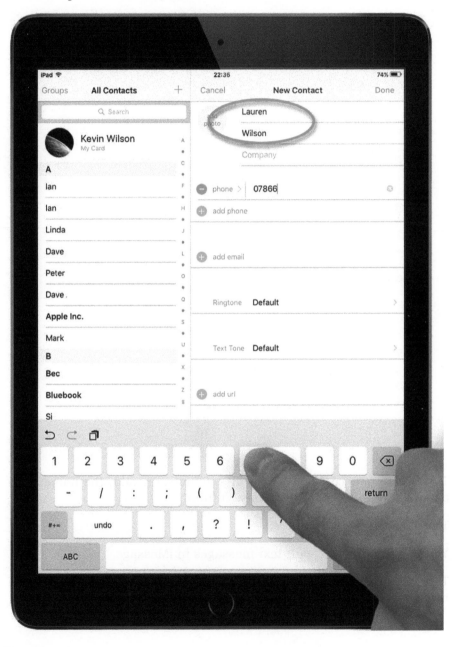

Tap 'done'.

You can also add a contact from an email message. Open the email message in the Mail App and tap on their name at the top of the email.

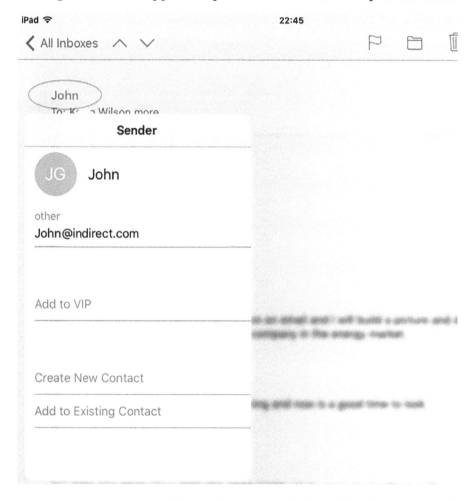

Tap 'create new contact'. iPad will automatically add, the names and email address the message was sent from.

Tap done.

You can do the same with text messages in iMessage.

Tap the message, tap 'details', tap the 'i' icon (top right), tap 'create new contact'. Enter their name and details in the screen that appears.

To view a contact's details, tap on the name. From here you can send a message, FaceTime them if they have it or give them a call.

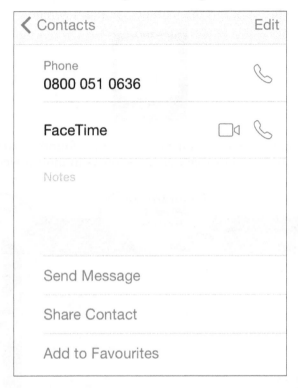

Tap 'edit' to amend any of their details.

Calendar (iCal)

To start calendar app, tap the icon on the main screen

This will bring up the calendar main screen. I found it easiest to view the calendar in month or week view. Below is in month view.

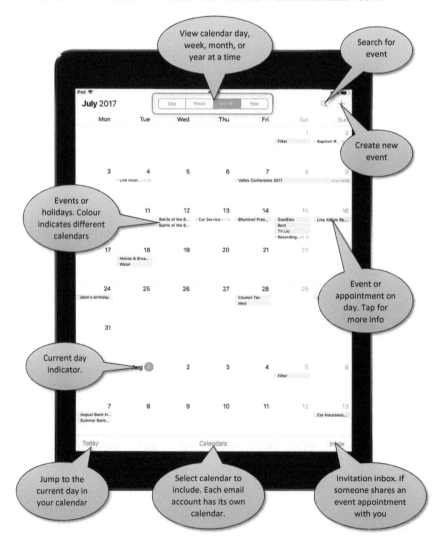

Adding an Appointment

To add an event to the calendar, tap and hold your finger on the day the event falls on.

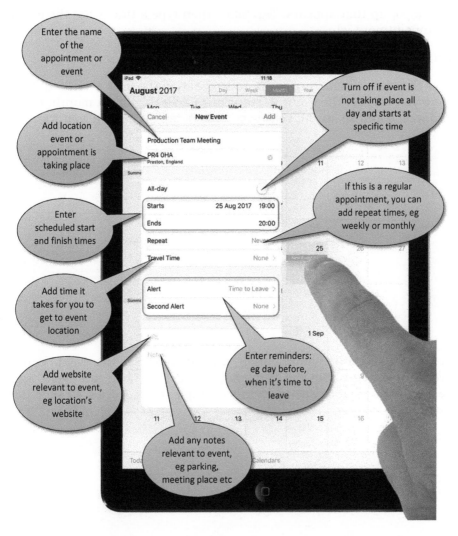

Enter the name of the appointment or event

Add location event or appointment is taking place

Enter scheduled start and finish times

Add time it takes for you to get to event location

Add website relevant to event, eg location's website

Turn off if event is not taking place all day and starts at specific time

If this is a regular appointment, you can add repeat times, eg weekly or monthly

Enter reminders: eg day before, when it's time to leave

Add any notes relevant to event, eg parking, meeting place etc

In the popup that appears. Tap 'title', then type a title (what the event or appointment is).

Do the same for location, and select your times.

Once you are finished tap done.

Add a Recurring Appointment

To add a recurring event to the calendar, tap and hold your finger on the first day the event falls on.

In the popup that appears. Tap 'title', then type a title (what the event or appointment is).

Do the same for location, and select your times.

Now to create a recurring event, tap 'repeat' in the 'new event' window. Here you can set the event to recur once a week, once a month, every two weeks and so on. All you have to do is tap on the one you want.

You can also set a custom option, tap 'custom'. Say the event occurs every three weeks. Set the frequency to 'weekly'. Then tap 'every' and select the number of weeks. In this example, three weeks, so slide the number to '3'.

Frequency	Weekly
Every	3 weeks

1	
2	
3	weeks
4	
5	

Once you are finished, tap 'repeat' on the top left of the repeat window to go back. Tap 'add' to add the event to your calendar.

Adding an Appointment from a Message

Apple Mail, iMessage and FaceTime will scan your message for phrases that look like dates and times and will create a link in the email for you. To add the event from the email or text message, tap on this link. From the popup box tap 'create event'.

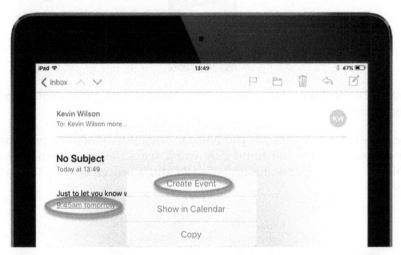

Enter a title and location if calendar didn't pick one up from the email. You can also tweak the information and add additional information if required.

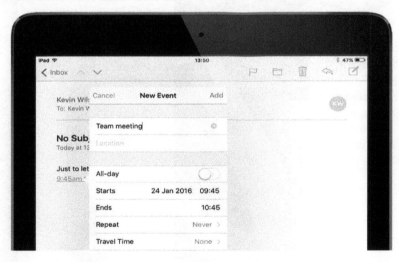

Once you have done that, tap 'add' to enter the appointment into your calendar.

101

FaceTime

To use FaceTime, tap the icon on the home screen. You will need your Apple ID and a wifi/data connection to the internet.

When you open FaceTime, you will be prompted to sign in if you haven't already done so.

Once FaceTime has opened, you'll see in the main window a preview of your camera. On the left hand side you'll see a darkened panel where you'll find your contacts, history of calls and a search for you to search for people

In this demonstration, Claire is going to facetime me from her iPad. Start typing the person's name you want to facetime into the search field on the top left of the screen. If the name is in your contacts, then it will appear underneath. Tap the little camera icon next to the name to make a facetime call.

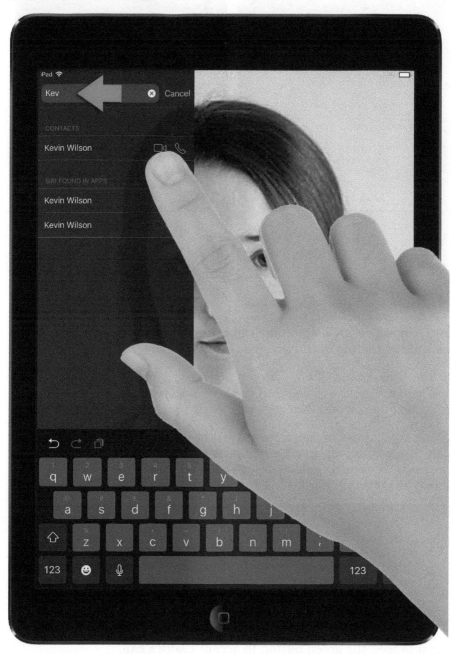

Wait for the other person to answer...

Claire's iPad is on the left in the demo below, and she is placing a facetime call to me on my iPad on the right.

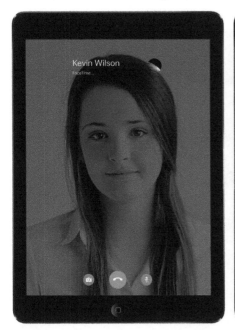 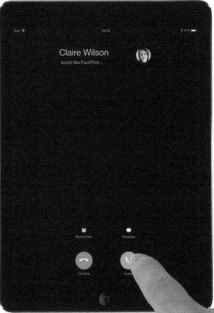

You can see on my iPad on the right, it tells me who is calling with the caller id at the top of the screen.

In the background of your screen you'll see a preview of your camera - so make sure you're squarely in the frame so when you answer your call, the other person can see you clearly.

Along the bottom of the screen you'll see a red button to decline the call. Tap 'remind me' to set a reminder to call back. If you can't talk tap 'message' to send a quick message such as 'on my way', 'can I call you later', or 'cant talk now'.

I just tapped the green button to accept Claire's call.

You can now have a video conversation with them. The onboard microphone on your iPhone/iPad will pick up your voice, so just talk naturally.

You'll see a picture of them in the centre of your screen with a thumbnail view of your own camera on the top right. Here's the view of Claire's call from my iPad.

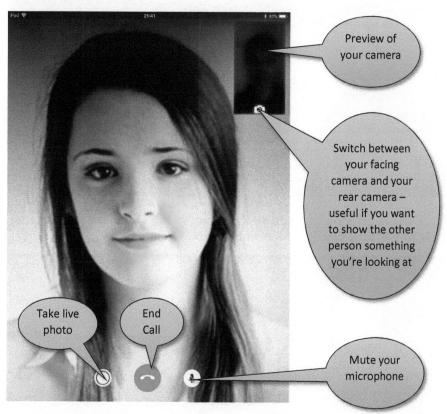

Along the bottom, you'll see three icons. If these icons disappear, tap the screen once and they'll re-appear. The white circle on the left takes a live photo, the red icon in the centre ends the call and the white mic icon on the right mutes your microphone.

It's a great tool to keep in touch with family, see the kids if you're away, and so they can see you too.

To add a contact, type their email address into the search field on the left hand side of the screen and tap on the email address that pops up below.

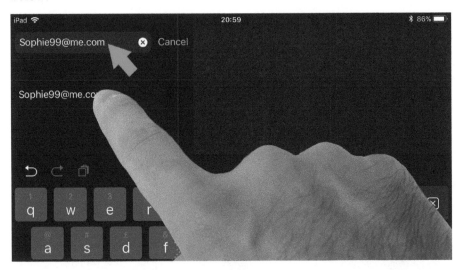

From the selections tap 'add new contact'. This will allow you to enter their name, address, phone numbers and so on.

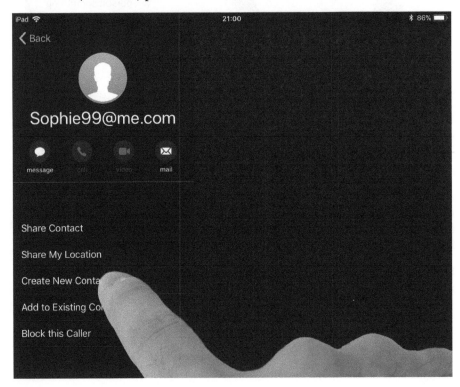

Enter the person's details into the correct fields.

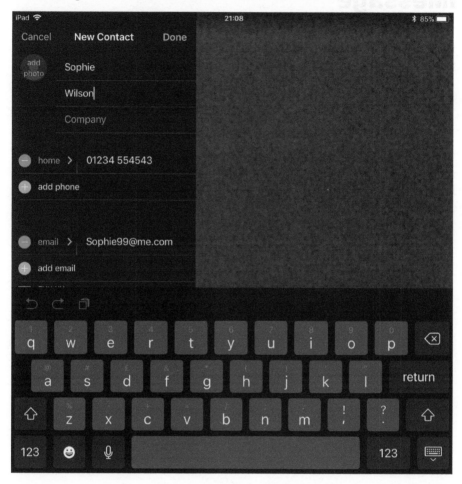

Tap in each field and add the information using the onscreen keyboard. You don't have to fill in every field, just the ones that are relevant.

Tap on 'add photo' on the top left. You can either take a photo using your camera, or select one from your photo library.

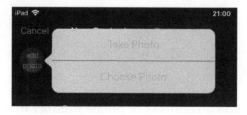

Tap 'done' when you're finished.

iMessage

You can send photos and videos and also voice messages to anyone with an apple device. To start iMessage, tap the icon on your home screen.

When you open iMessage, you will see a list of all your received messages. Tap on a message to read and reply. Tap the new message icon on the top of the messages list on the left hand pane.

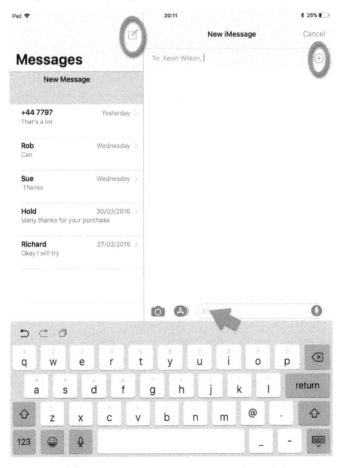

Tap the + sign to add an address or phone number from your contacts.

Type your message in the box indicated with the red arrow.

You can send a voice message by tapping and holding your finger on the mic icon. Record your message, then release your finger to stop.

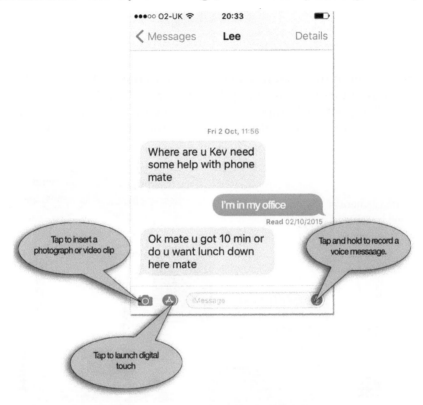

From the options that appear, select from the icons below.

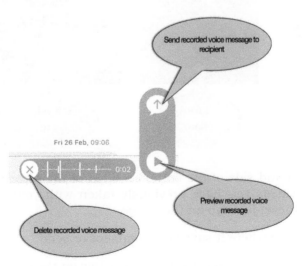

To send a photograph or video, tap the small camera icon on the bottom left of your message window.

At the bottom of the screen, you'll see two sections. On the left hand side is your camera, point at anything you want to take a photograph to send. The photo will appear automatically in the message window. Tap the small white circle at the bottom of the camera preview to take the photograph.

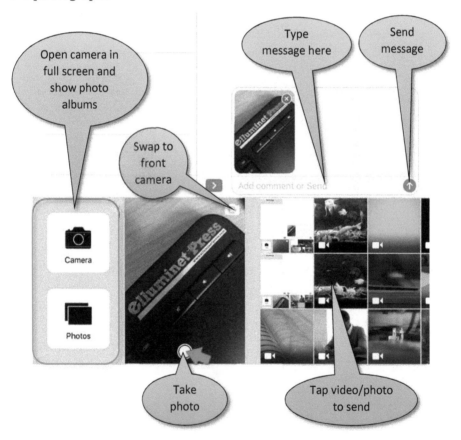

On the right hand side of the bottom section of the screen, you'll see photos and videos you have previously taken with your camera. To send any of these, just tap on the image.

Enter a message where it says 'add comment or send'.

To send the message, tap the small blue arrow on the right hand side.

Digital Touch in iMessage

In digital touch mode, you can draw with your finger and send animations.

Tap the store icon to the left side of the text field to reveal additional options. Then tap the digital touch icon.

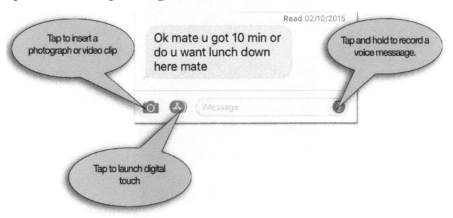

This opens up the digital touch interface. Make sure you select the digital touch icon on the bottom left. Tap the red circle on the left hand side.

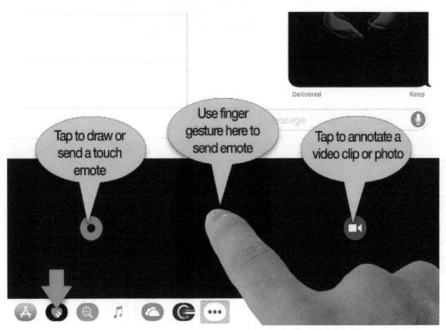

This will allow you to use certain finger gestures to send different emotes. For example, you can use one finger to draw or write something, press with one finger to send a fireball effect, tap with two fingers to send a kiss and so on. Here's a list of a few of the good ones...

You can also draw using your finger, tap on a colour along the left hand side, then draw a diagram on the black screen in the centre. Press on a colour to open up the colour wheel if the colour you want isn't listed.

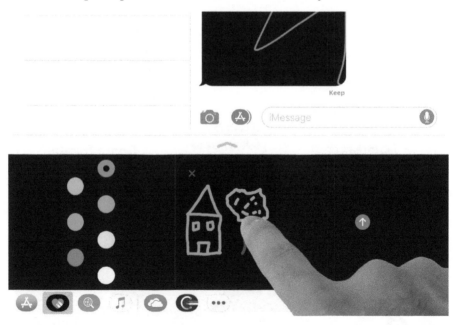

Tap on the blue arrow to the right to send.

You can also annotate a video or photograph using digital touch. To do this, from digital touch interface, tap the camera icon.

Tap the red button to start recording. While the video is recording, use the digital touch tools to draw on it. Tap a colour, then draw or write on the image with your finger.

The white button at the bottom left takes a photo, while the red button in the centre records a video.

Try a few 'tap and holds' with two fingers to add a few hearts. Or tap with two fingers to send a kiss.

Tap the record button again to stop recording. Tap the blue arrow at the bottom right to send your finished piece.

You can also share gifs which are short animations. Select the digital touch icon circled below. Then along the bottom of the screen, select the 'search gif' icon. Tap on a gif to add it to your message or type in to the 'find images' field to search for something specific.

You can also share what music you are listening to on iTunes. Select the digital touch icon circled below. Then along the bottom of the screen, select the 'iTunes' icon.

You'll see all the music you have been listening to or currently listening to on your iPad. Tap on a track to share.

Sending Payments with iMessage

Introduced in this version of iOS is the ability to send payments to contacts on iMessage using Apple Pay. This only work between apple devices at the moment, so you can't send payments to users of other phones or tablets.

Tap the store icon to the left side of the text field to reveal additional options. Then tap the Apple Pay icon.

If you have Apple Pay set up on your iPad, you'll see an extra icon at the bottom.

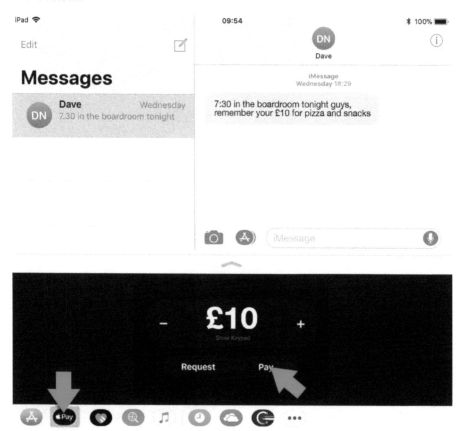

Enter the amount. Either use the + and - buttons to increase/decrease the amount, or tap 'show keypad' to tap in the amount. Once you're don'e hit 'pay'.

If people are owing you money, you can enter the amount as above and tap 'request' to send them an invite to pay you the amount.

AirDrop

AirDrop allows you to transfer files from one device to another using bluetooth wireless technology.

To use AirDrop you will need a compatible device, such as the iPhone 5 or later, fourth-generation iPad, iPad mini, and fifth-generation iPod touch, and have both Bluetooth and Wi-Fi enabled.

Swipe your finger upwards from the bottom edge of your screen, to open control center. Turn on Wi-Fi and Bluetooth.

To enable AirDrop open Control Centre and press the AirDrop icon. Make yourself discoverable to just those in your contacts.

Be careful if you select 'everyone' as this means anyone in that has an airdrop enabled device can connect and send files to your device, which could be a possible security risk.

To Send a file to Someone using AirDrop

You can send a file or photo from iphone to another iphone or another ipad.

In this example, I am going to send a photo. So launch Photos app.

Tap the image or video you want to share from your albums, tap next.

Tap on the Share button. AirDrop will detect other devices in the vicinity. In this example, AirDrop has detected my iPhone. This is the one I want to share with.

Tap the icon of the person/device you want to send to.

118

Now when you send the photo, the other person will get a prompt to download the image. Accept the confirmation and your image will download.

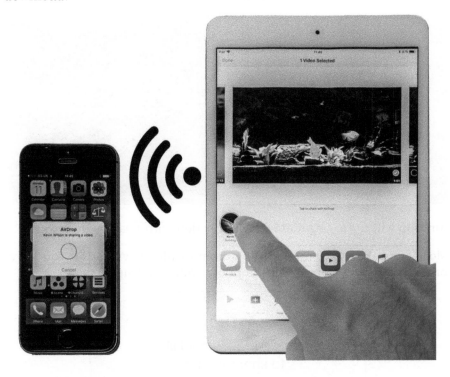

The image/video will be added to your photo library. The photo sent has appeared in photos app on the iPhone.

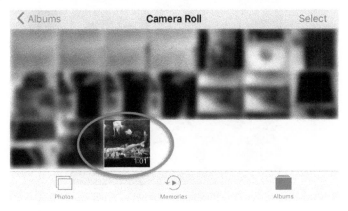

This works the same for other files too, just select the file and tap the share icon. Files will appear in the relevant apps; music will go to iTunes and files will be stored in Files app. If iOS doesn't recognise the file type, then it will ask you what app you want to open the file with.

To Receive a File from Someone using AirDrop

Make sure your AirDrop is enabled on your device.

AirDrop will try to negotiate the connection with near by devices.

More often than not, the file will automatically download. If you get a prompt, tap on Accept when the photo comes through

Go into your photos app and the photo will be stored in there.

120

Chapter 4

Using Multimedia

Your iPad is a multimedia rich device, meaning you can take photos and record videos. You can even edit and enhance your photos, correct colour and brightness.

You can post your photographs to your favourite social media account for the world to see.

You can create slideshows, edit your videos, download and watch TV programmes and films.

You can download and play any kind of music you can think of, all from your iPad.

So lets begin by taking a look at the Photos App.

Photos

Using the photos app, you can import photos from a memory card or store, edit and share photos taken with the on board cameras on your iPad.

Import Photos

There are two adapters available to accomplish this: the Lightning to USB Camera Adapter, or the Lightning to SD Card Reader.

The card reader enables you to insert the SD card from your camera and copy images from it.

The card reader plugs into the docking port on the bottom of the iPad. Launch the iPhoto app. Tap on camera or card.

Chapter 4: Using Multimedia

You can also connect your camera directly using a lightning to USB connector. Plug the connector into the bottom of your iPad, then plug the USB cable that came with your camera into the other end of the lightning to USB adapter.

When iPad detects your media, it will prompt you with an import screen. Tap the photographs you want to import and then tap import to copy the photos across.

Once the photos have been imported, you will be prompted asking you whether to keep the images or delete them.

If you select keep, this leaves all the photos intact on the memory card. If you select delete, this deletes the photos you just imported off the memory card.

Editing Photos

You can do some basic editing on your iPad. You can lighten up dark images, crop and rotate your photos.

To do this tap on the photograph in the photos app.

The image will open up full screen. Tap on the edit icon on the top right of the screen.

Along the bottom of the screen you'll see your editing icons.

Reading the icons in the centre from left to right we have:

Image enhance, this automatically selects the brightness, colour and contrast settings for your photograph. Most of the time it is a guess based on optimal settings but doesn't always get it right.

Image crop and rotate, this allows you to rotate images that may have been taken at an angle or crop parts of the photo you don't want.

Effects, allows you to add black and white, fade, sepia effects to a photo.

Adjustments, allows you to adjust colour, brightness, contrast, bring up shadows, reduce highlights in bright areas of a photo

Crop and Rotate an Image

You can crop an image by tapping on the crop image icon, circled below, and dragging the crop box around the bit of the photo you want.

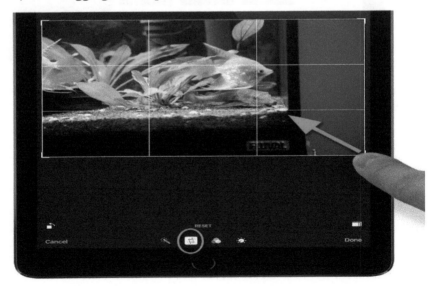

If you want to rotate the image, tap and drag the rotation protractor underneath the image to the left or right.

If you want to correct colour, contrast or brightness, tap the adjustments icon, circled below.

In this example I am going to adjust the brightness of the photo. So tap on 'light'.

The 'light' group contains everything to do with exposure: brightness, contrast, highlights, shadows etc.

Drag the slider with your finger, left and right, to adjust the brightness. To change contrast or highlights, tap the hamburger icon to the right.

From the menu, select the one you want to change - try adjusting highlights - this is the bright parts of the image. Also try adjust the contrast.

Use the slider to change the setting.

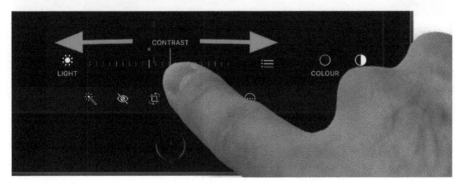

Taking Pictures with Camera App

Tap the camera icon on the home screen.

You can use your iPad as a camera to take photos and record video.

Along the right side of your screen you have some icons. With the top icon, you can enable HDR (this is good for scenes where you have dark shadows and bright areas such as sky). Next down is a timer delay (can set to off, 3 or 10 seconds). Third icon down swaps between front and rear camera. The white circle takes the photo, the thumbnail icon underneath shows you the last photo taken. Underneath this you can select the type of video or photo you want to take: time lapse, slomo, video, photo, square photo and panoramic photo. You can select them by swiping your finger over them.

You can adjust the zoom using the slider on the left hand side of the image. Drag the circle on the bar upwards to zoom in, and downwards to zoom out.

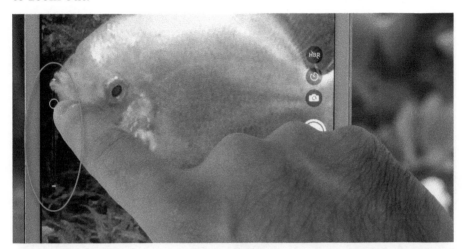

If you're having trouble focusing, tap and hold your finger on the object you want to focus on. This will lock the exposure and focus on that object, so it doesn't change, making it easier to take the photo.

Tap the white circle on the right hand side as normal to take the photo

You can also adjust the brightness before you take a photo. To do this tap on the screen and you'll see a yellow square show up with a vertical line with a slider on it.

Drag the slider upward to brighten up the image, slide it downward to darken the image.

Tap the white circle to take the photo as normal.

Once you have taken your photo you can you can crop or rotate the image. Rotating an image is good for straightening up photos.

To crop the image, tap the photo icon on the right hand side of the screen, to open the photo you just took.

Use the grid shown below to highlight the section of the photograph you want to keep. Drag the edges of the box inwards to the point you want to crop

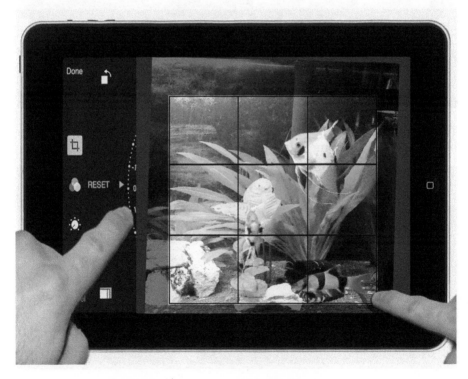

You can straighten a photograph by rotating it a number of degrees. To do this drag the dials up and down on the left hand side of the screen.

You can also change the shading and tonal effects of the image, making your image black and white, a sepia effect or boost the colours.

Tap the photo icon on the right hand side of the screen, to open the photo you just took.

Now tap edit on the top right of your screen. To add tonal effects, tap the colour icon at the bottom of your screen.

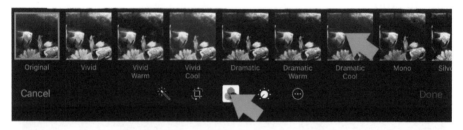

You can adjust the brightness and contrast or highlight shadows where photographs have come out dark in places.

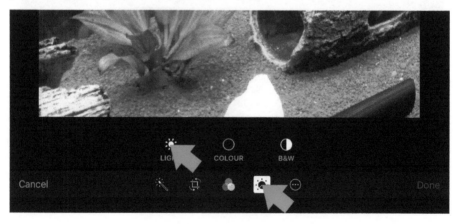

You can do this by tapping on the light adjust icon. This is the same as adjusting your photos in the photos app.

From the options, select the attributes of the photo you want to adjust, this is the exposure, highlights, shadows, brightness, contrast, or black point.

For example, tap on highlights to darken some of the bright parts in your image.

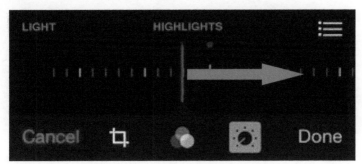

Drag the bar left and right to change the highlight.

Also try exposure or brightness to lighten a dark image or shadows to lighten up dark parts of an image.

Panoramic Photos

Panoramic shots are great for scenery and landscapes. Photos app allows you to automatically take a series of photos and it stitches them together into a long panoramic image.

To take panoramic photos, open your camera app, select pano from the right hand side of the screen. You might need to scroll down the selections if it isn't visible.

Now, move your iPad to the start of the scene and tap the white circle. You'll notice in the centre of the screen a rectangular box, this will start to fill as you move your iPad across the scene. In this demonstration, I'm taking a panoramic photo of a mountain range.

Position your iPad camera at the beginning of the mountain range on the left, tap the white 'take photo' icon on the right of your screen. Now move your camera along the mountain range until you get to the end. You'll see the rectangular box in the centre of the screen fill up as you do so. Tap the white circle again to finish. Make sure you stand in one spot, the panoramic photos don't work if you walk along with it.

Recording Video

You can record video using the camera app. Select 'video' from the list on the bottom right of your screen.

To take the best looking video, use your iPad in a horizontal orientation as shown below.

Tap the red circle icon on the right hand side of the screen to start recording. Tap on any part of the screen to focus on that point during the video. Use the slider on the left hand side to zoom in and out. Tap the red circle icon on the right hand side to stop recording.

Live Photos

Live Photos capture 1.5 seconds of motion before and after the photo.

To take a live photo, from the Camera app, tap the Live Photo button, right at the top of the screen to turn it on, indicated with the red arrow below.

Tap the Shutter button to take your Live Photo.

They animate when you press firmly and hold your finger on the photo. To see your live photos in the photos app, tap on the photo thumbnail in the main screen.

Then when the photo opens up, press your finger firmly on the photo to see the animation.

Share Pics on Social Media

You will need to be logged into, and downloaded the appropriate app from the app store; facebook or twitter etc.

In this example I'm going to share a photograph on Facebook of the twins.

If you have taken the photo using your camera, tap the small thumbnail in the bottom right hand corner. *If you're in the photos app, tap on your photograph thumbnail to open it in edit mode.*

Once the photo opens up, tap the share icon in the top right corner.

Select 'Facebook' from the list of social media icons.

Chapter 4: Using Multimedia

Type a message in your post, then hit 'post'.

You can use the same procedure for Twitter, email iMessage and any other social media you use. Just select the icon from the social media icons list

Music with iTunes

You can start the music app by tapping on music icon on the main screen.

Once music app has loaded you can see all the albums that are currently on your iPad

Tapping on the album cover brings up the song list. Just tap the song on the song list and it will start playing. Time to put on your headphones.

Transferring Music from your Computer

To get music onto iPad you can purchase and download from the iTunes Store or sync with iTunes on your computer, by connecting your iPad using the iPad cable.

Open iTunes on your computer and click the iPad/iPhone icon on the top left of the tool bar.

Here you can update your iPad's iOS software, just click 'check for update'. Press the option key and click 'check for updates' if you have downloaded a restore image (IPSW).

You can restore your device to its factory settings if you have problems with it. To do this click 'restore iPhone/iPad'. This will wipe your data, apps, music and settings, so you'll need to restore from a backup if you do this.

Further down the options, you can set backups. By default, your data is automatically backed up to your iCloud account, but you can also set it to backup to your computer - this means you'd have to plug your device into your computer to allow this. Most of the time leaving this backing up to iCloud is sufficient.

Scroll down to the bottom of this page and select 'manually manage music and videos'. This allows you to select the songs or albums you want to transfer instead of syncing your whole library.

Once you have done that, enable your sidebar in iTunes. I find this helps when transferring songs or albums to an iPad

You can do this by going to the view menu and selecting show sidebar.

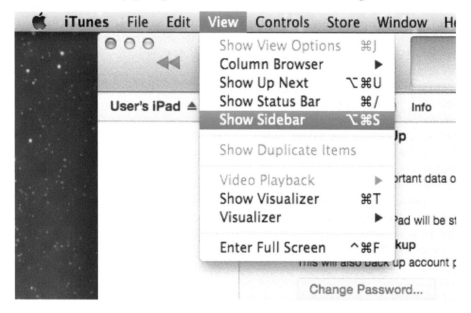

Now select your music library from the top left.

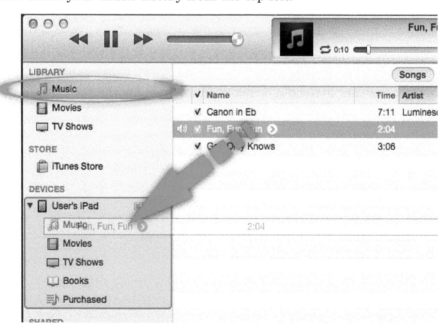

To add any music to your iPad, just drag and drop the track or album onto the iPad device shown in the left hand sidebar.

iTunes Store

You can start the iTunes store by tapping on the icon on your home screen

Once the app has loaded you can browse through music, movies and tv shows by tapping on the icons. You can also type what you are looking for in the search field on the top right of the screen.

To buy any of the tracks or albums, tap your finger on the price tag.

You will need your apple id to buy any of the media.

147

Apple Music

Apple Music is a music streaming service and for a monthly subscription fee, you can listen to any music that is available in the iTunes Store.

£9.99 a month gets you full access to the iTunes store and many radio stations available. This is an individual account and allows only one account access to the iTunes Store.

£14.99 a month gets you full access to the iTunes store and radio stations and allows up to 6 people to sign in and listen to their music. This is ideal for families.

To get started, make sure you have updated to the latest iTunes on your iPad. Tap the Music App on your home screen.

From the Apple Music's main screen, tap the account icon in the top left corner. From the screen that appears, choose 'join apple music'

Choose a membership programme and sign in with your Apple ID

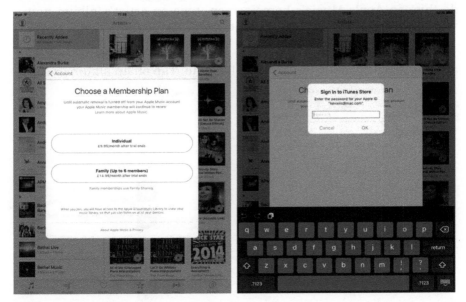

Select the genres you like. If you don't see the ones you like, tap the magnifying glass icon on the top right and search. Tap next.

Select the artists you like. If you don't see the ones you like, tap the magnifying glass icon on the top right and search for their name. Tap Done.

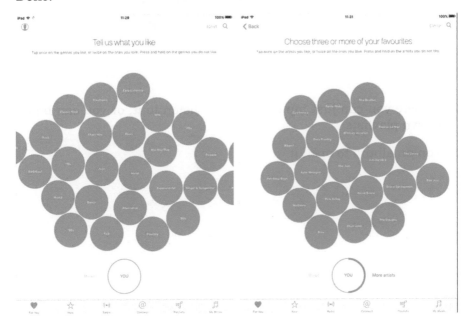

Now, you can search for any artist, band or song you can think of. To do this, on Apple Music's home screen, type an artist's/album name into the search field on the top right.

Tap on the name in the search list. You will see a whole selection of albums, singles and songs you can listen to. Tap on an album or song.

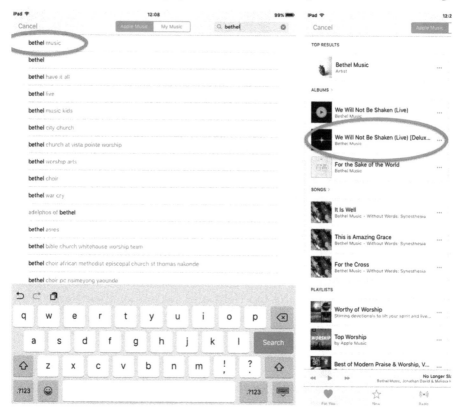

From here you can just tap on a song to listen to it, or you can build your own playlists.

Tap on an album to open it.

From the drop down menu that appears, select 'add to playlist'

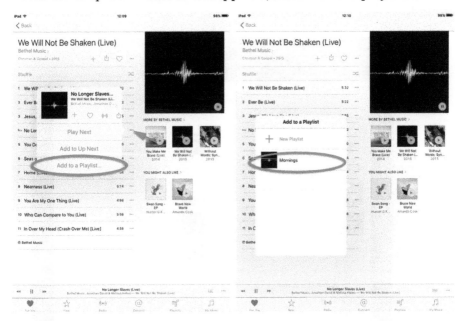

Then select your playlist you want to add your song to. If you have no playlists, tap 'new playlist' and give it a name.

Tap done.

Chapter 4: Using Multimedia

You can use the icons along the bottom of Apple Music to navigate around.

Videos

Your iPad has a built in app for videos but is designed to stream TV shows and films to your device. You can also download YouTube to watch videos online.

Videos App

The idea is, you buy or rent the programme or film from the iTunes store.

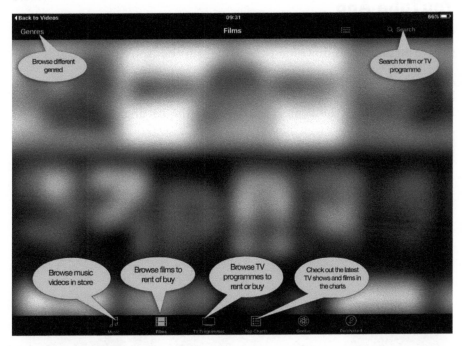

You can also search for a specific title using the search field at the top of the screen. To buy or rent any item, tap on the thumbnail, then on the screen that appears, tap rent or buy.

Chapter 4: Using Multimedia

Your videos will appear on the app's main screen. Tap on a thumbnail to watch the video.

YouTube App

YouTube is probably the most common way to watch videos on your iPad. You'll need to download the app from the App Store.

Along the top of the main screen, in the centre, you have your home button, hot and trending topics, your youtube account details. On the far right you have the search button, and the settings button.

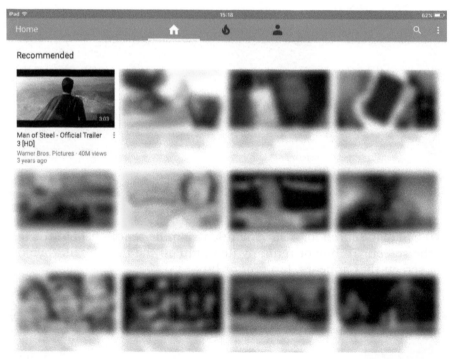

Tap on an image thumbnail to view the video. You can search by tapping on the magnifying glass icon, on the top right of the screen. Enter your search.

Airplay

Airplay allows wireless streaming of audio and video data to an Apple TV or compatible receiver on your TV.

For this to work, both your iPad and Apple TV will need to be on the same WiFi network.

To mirror your iPad, open your command centre by double pressing your home button.

Tap on 'screen mirroring' or 'airplay mirroring' and select your Apple TV from the list. Enter your passcode if prompted.

If you don't know the Apple TV passcode, go on your Apple TV, then go to settings > Airplay, select 'Onscreen code'.

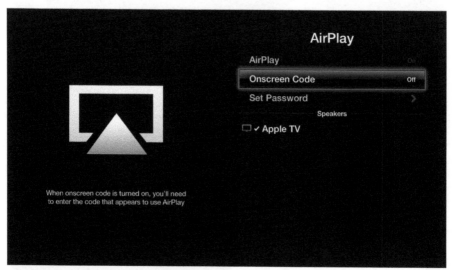

You can turn off the code or set a new one.

Using Apple Pencil

This is only really available on the iPad Pro models and requires you to buy a digital pen stylus.

First you should charge up your pencil. To do this, pull the small white cap off the back of your pencil.

Plug the pencil into the lightning port on the bottom on your iPad. Leave it plugged in for a short while to give it some charge.

Chapter 4: Using Multimedia

Open up an app such as the notes app or concepts app. In this example, I am using the concepts drawing app which is available from the app store.

You can draw directly onto the surface of your iPad. Tilt your pen to the side and you can shade in areas.

Press harder to darken or thicken the lines

You can also highlight and annotate using your favourite productivity apps. In Microsoft Word, select the 'draw' ribbon, select a pen and draw directly onto the document.

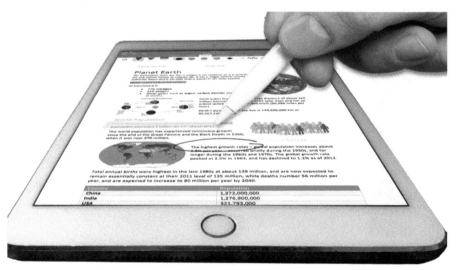

Document Scanner

Within the Notes App, you can scan documents and convert them. From the Notes App, tap the + sign on the bottom right of your screen.

Tap 'manual' on the right hand side, this is so you can take a photo of each of your pages and gives you more control than auto mode.

Line up the document in the window as shown below, make sure the yellow box covers the whole document.

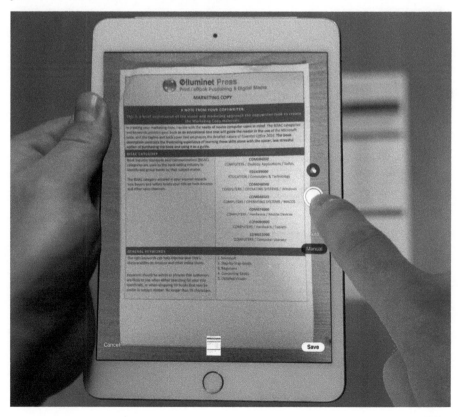

Tap the white button on the right hand side to 'scan the document'. If you have more pages, repeat the process and 'scan' them as well using the white button on the right hand side. Once you have 'scanned' all your pages, tap 'save' on the bottom right corner.

The pages will be added to your note. Tap on the thumbnail to open it up full screen.

Now you can send the document via email, safe it as a PDF, print it and write directly onto the scan with markup.

Tap the 'share' icon on the top right of your screen.

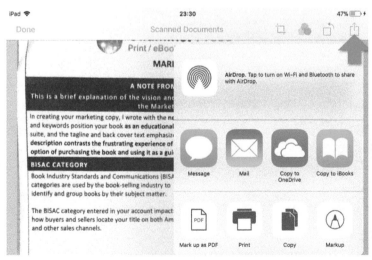

In this demonstration, I'm going to add some annotations with the markup tool. So tap 'markup'.

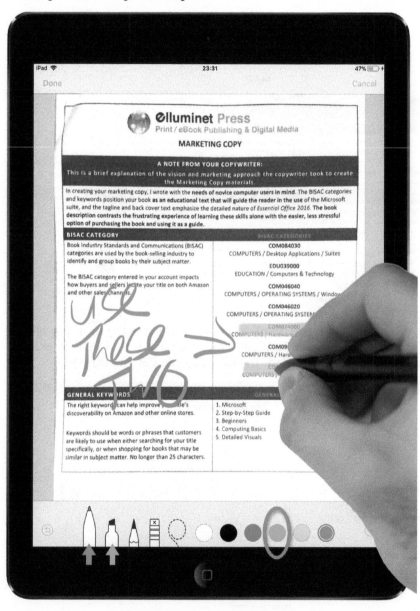

Select a pen or highlighter from the selection at the bottom left, and select a colour from the bottom right. Use your finger or pen to draw directly onto the scanned document.

When you're done, tap done on the top left.

Now to send it or save it, tap the 'share' icon on the top right of the screen.

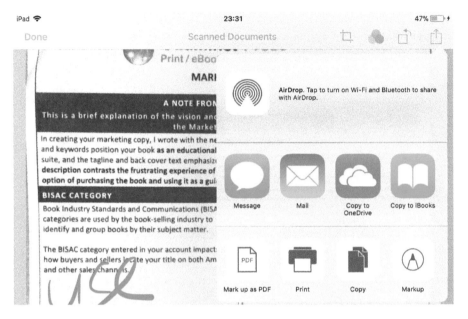

From the drop down, tap 'mail' to email it to someone or 'message' to send via iMessage. From here you can also save it to a PDF or print it if you have air print installed. In this example I'm emailing it.

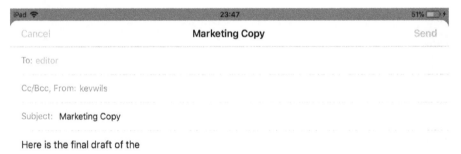

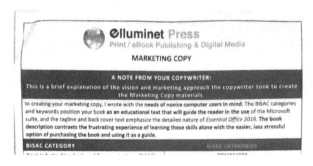

QR Code Scanner

Open your camera app, point it at a QR code, tap the code on the screen to focus.

When the camera reads the code, you'll see a prompt at the top of the screen telling you what the code is and where it links to. Tap and drag the small handle, circled above, down to expand the window to see a preview of the website. Tap on the site to open it up in full screen.

Common Apps

You can pretty much get an app for virtually anything, and these are all available from the app store. Some are free and others you have to buy.

There are games, productivity apps and apps just for fun.

Your iPad comes with some apps build in but you can download millions more from the App Store.

Lets start by taking a look at the App Store in more detail.

The App Store has had a make over in this version of iOS and has a much easier to use interface

App Store

The app store has over 1 million apps available for download direct to your iPad without even going on a computer. To start app store, click App Store app on your main screen.

Once on the app store's main screen, tap the icon on the top right to sign in with your apple id if you haven't already done so. If you are already signed in, your apple id will be displayed here, you won't need to sign in again.

Apps

TRY SOMETHING NEW
Bloom - Colouring Book
Your real world colour palette

TRY SOMETHING NEW
Farfetch – Shop & Discover Desig...   B
Shop the latest trends   W

In the box that appears, enter your apple id details.

	Account	Done
Apple ID	Email	
Password	Required	
Sign In		
	Forgot your Apple ID or password?	

Chapter 5: Common Apps

On the app store, you will find everything from games and entertainment to productivity tools such as word processing, drawing and photo apps.

These are split into games and app sections and you'll find these on the bar along the bottom of the screen.

Also along the bottom you'll find updates to your installed apps, it's worth checking this from time to time, as apps are updated all the time.

The last icon on the bar along the bottom allows you to search the app store for a specific app name or type/genre of app.

You can even find apps for recipes, travel details, maps. There is an app for almost anything you can think of.

Search for Apps

To find an app, tap on 'search' on the bar at the bottom of your screen. Type into the search field on the main screen, as shown below. In this example, I'm going to search for one of my favourite games called 'worms'.

From the suggestions, tap on the closest match. Tap on the image to view more details about the app; here you'll see reviews, price, screen shots and other info.

To download the app, tap 'get' next to the app if it's free, or tap the price if it's paid.

Chapter 5: Common Apps

If it's a paid app, tap 'purchase to confirm.

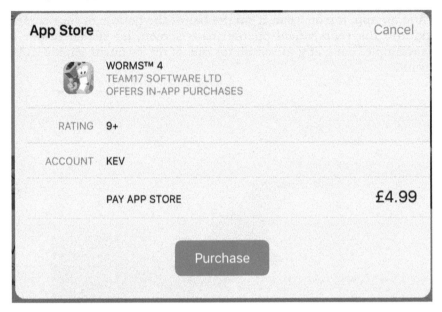

Authorise the purchase with your password or thumb print.

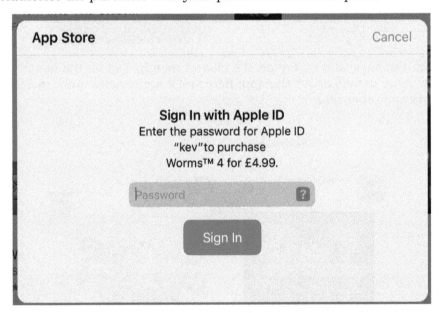

The app will appear on your home screen once it has downloaded and installed itself.

Browsing the Store

If you are more the browsing type, app store has grouped all the apps into categories according to their use. Select 'apps' from the bar on the bottom of the screen. Here you'll see some of the most popular apps, new apps and top selling apps. You can tap on any of these apps to view or download.

Tap on the app's image to view more details, Tap 'see all' at the top of each section to see all the apps in that section. Tap on 'get' or the price to download the app. Scroll down the page to see all the apps in the sections.

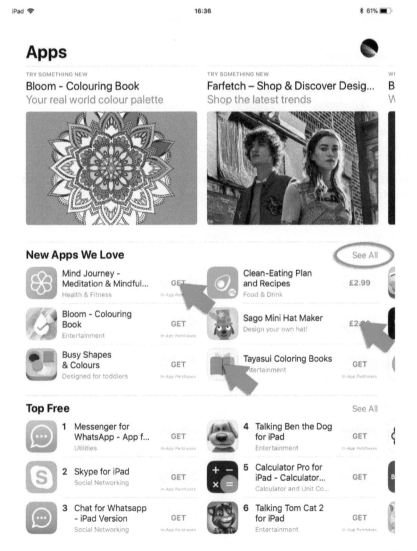

Chapter 5: Common Apps

If you scroll down a bit, you'll see a section called 'top categories'.

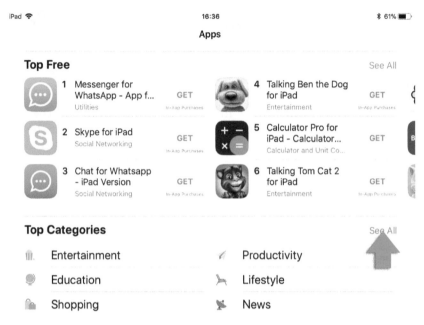

Tap on a category to browse the available apps. In this example, I'm going to explore the 'reference' category.

Here, you'll see a list of all the apps available for that category. Again, tap 'see all' on the top right to see the full lists in the different sections.

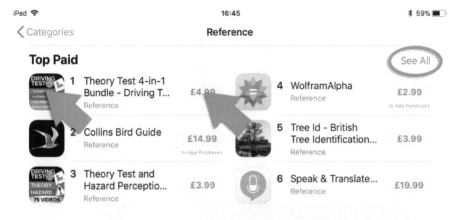

Claire is 18 and learning to drive, so two apps might be of use to her: Theory Test and Hazard Perception. Tap on the apps icon to view more details about the app

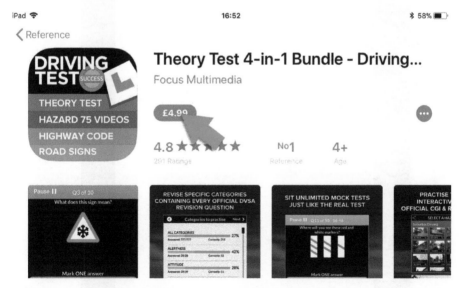

Tap the price to download the and install the app on your iPad

This gives you information about what the app does, what it costs, some screen shots of the app in action and the device requirements in order to run the app.

To purchase an app, just tap on the price tag.

Taking Notes

To start notes app, tap on the icon on the home screen.

When notes has loaded, you can view your saved notes along the left hand side. You can add a new note by tapping the pen and pad icon on the top right.

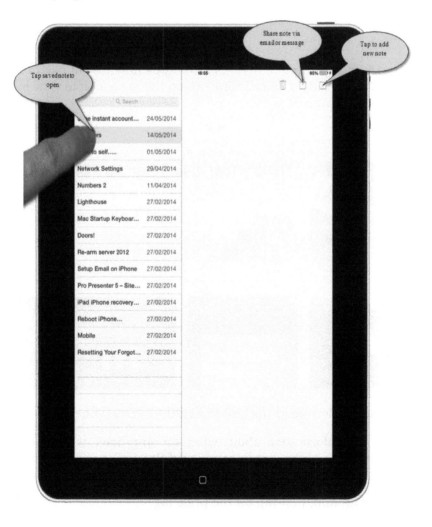

Typing Notes & Inserting Photos

You can type your notes in as if it were a notepad, using the on screen keyboard.

You can also insert a photograph by tapping on the small camera icon.

Dictating Notes

Instead of typing, you can dictate notes using the voice dictation feature. To do this, tap the mic icon on the keyboard.

Record your notes using the voice recognition.

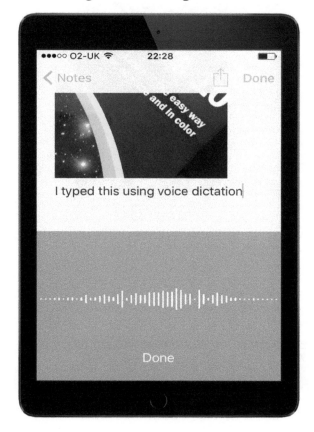

Tap done at the bottom, when you are finished.

Reminders

To start reminders app, tap on the icon on the home screen

Add a Reminder

To add one, tap reminders (on the left hand side), tap on a blank line on the paper then type your reminder.

Tap return on the keyboard to add another reminder. These are reminders of things to do today.

175

Schedule a Reminder

To schedule reminders, tap scheduled on the left hand side of the screen

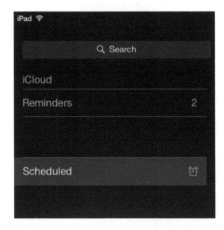

Add a reminder by tapping on a blank line and entering a description of the task.

Then tap the 'i' icon on the right hand side of the reminder

This will allow you to enter the date and time. Tap 'alarm' then swipe up and down the days and times that appear, shown below.

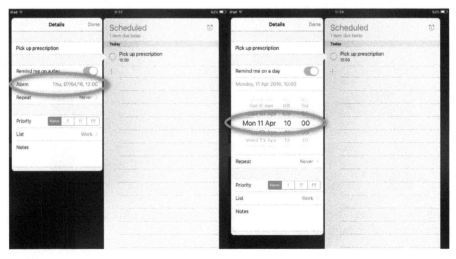

Maps

Maps can be extremely useful if you are trying to find out where a particular place is and need to find driving directions. It works almost like a satnav/gps giving you precise directions straight from door to door.

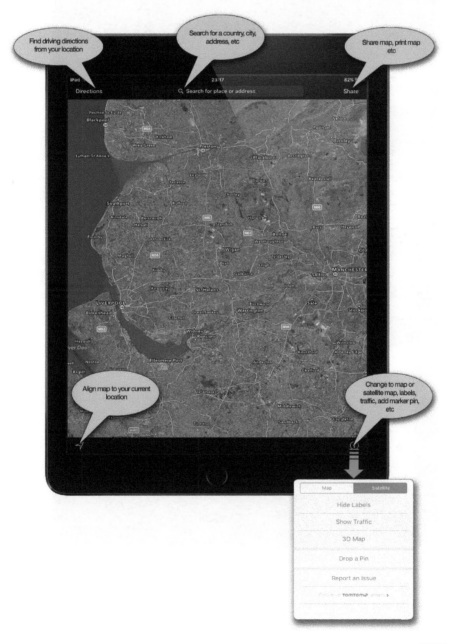

You can find driving directions by tapping the directions icon on the maps main screen. In the menu that appears enter your destination address in the end field. Then tap route when done.

You will see a list of turn by turn directions and your route will he highlighted in blue on the map

Tap start to begin your navigation.

Here you will see your turn by turn directions, these will change as you're driving a long.

You can also swipe across the instruction at the top of the screen to browse through the instructions. Not a good idea to do while you're driving though.

News App

The news app collects breaking stories from around the world and locally into one app, based on the topics you are interested in.

When you first start the app, need to pick your favourite sources; so things that might interest you such as sport, news, technology, favourite magazines and newspapers.

To select them, tap on the thumbnails.

Chapter 5: Common Apps

Scroll down, tap on a news story, or select from the tools at the bottom of the screen, as shown below.

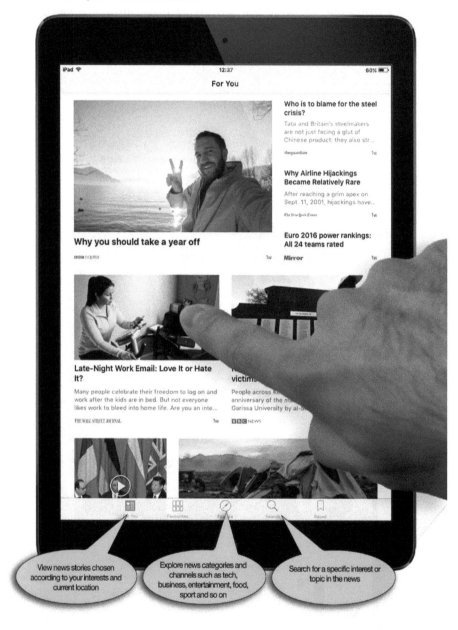

View news stories chosen according to your interests and current location

Explore news categories and channels such as tech, business, entertainment, food, sport and so on

Search for a specific interest or topic in the news

iBooks App

iBooks is your electronic bookshelf. Tap the icon on your home screen

You can download hundreds of different e-books that are available in the bookstore; from the latest novels, food, kids books or manuals.

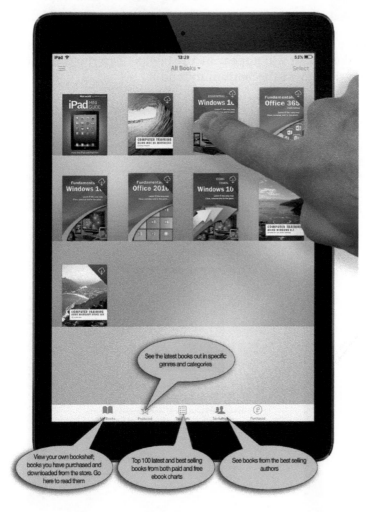

If you are searching for specific books, tap on 'featured', on the bar along the bottom.

In the search field on the top right corner, type the title of the book you're looking for.

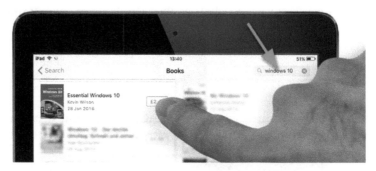

Tap on the price to purchase and download the title. Once the book has downloaded, it will appear in 'my books'. Tap the thumbnail in 'my books' on the bar at the bottom to read it.

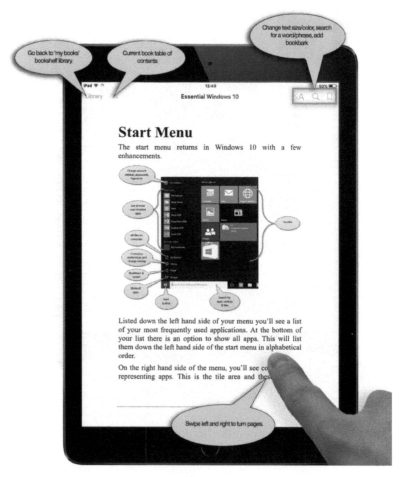

Files App

The iCloud Drive App has been dropped and replaced with the Files App. You'll find the icon on your dock, as shown below.

In the Files App, you'll find all your files that are stored on your iPad and iCloud Drive. Here is the Files App opened in horizontal mode.

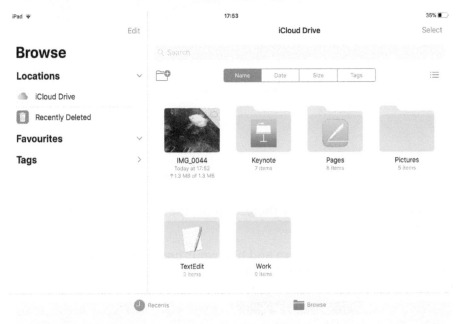

When working with any of Apple's productivity apps such as Keynote, Pages or Numbers, the files you create will be saved into the appropriate folders in the Files App.

You can also create your own folders. To do this tap the 'new folder' icon on the top left.

Chapter 5: Common Apps

You can drag and drop files into these folders. Tap and hold your finger on the icon, then drag your finger across the glass to the folder you want to put the file into.

Tap on the folders to open them, tap on the file thumbnails to open the files.

You can also delete files. Tap and hold your finger on the file thumbnail and from the pop up menu tap 'delete'.

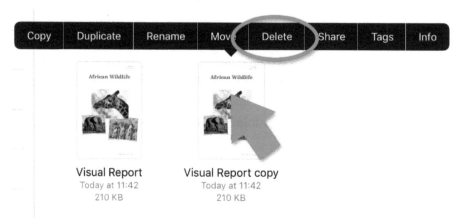

As an example, I am going to save a document from the Pages App. To make sure you're saving into iCloud Drive, from the start screen, tap 'location' on the top left. From the drop down select 'browse'.

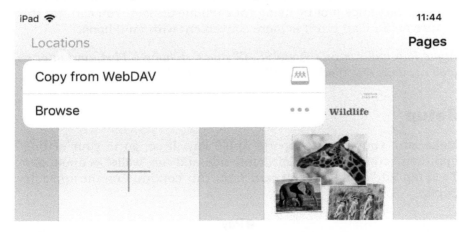

Tap 'locations', then tap 'iCloud Drive. Tap 'browse'.

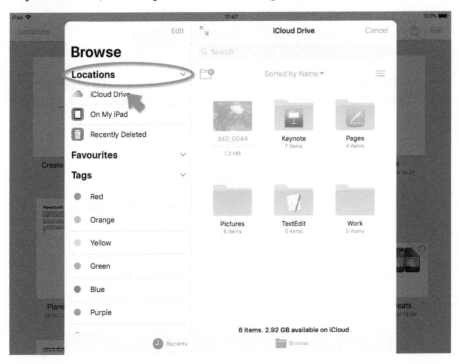

Tap the 'Pages' folder. Now you'll see all the files that have been saved in this folder.

'Pages' files are automatically saved here.

Apple Pay

Apple Pay allows you to keep digital copies of your bank cards, and lets you pay for things just by using your iPhone or iPad. You can use this feature on an iPad but it is more convenient with an iPhone.

Apple Pay will run on iPhone SE, iPhone 6, iPhone 6 Plus, and later as well as, iPad Pro, iPad Air 2, iPad mini 3, and later.

Setup

Make sure your bank supports Apple Pay. If so, go to your settings app then scroll down the left hand side and tap 'wallet & apple pay'. Then tap 'add credit or debit card' link. Tap 'continue' on the apple pay popup.

Now, in the 'add card' window, if you already have a credit/debit card registered with your apple id, then apple pay will ask you to add this one.

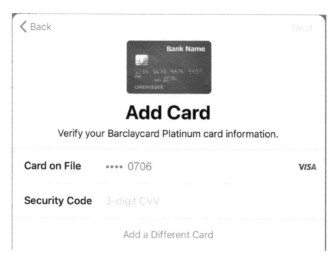

If this is the card you want to use, then enter the 3 digit security code and tap 'next' on the top right. Hit 'agree' on the terms and conditions; your card will be added.

188

If you want to add a different card, tap 'add a different card', at the bottom of the 'add card' window. You can scan your card with the iPad's camera.

Position the card so it fills the white rectangle on your screen. Apple Pay will scan your card and automatically enter your details

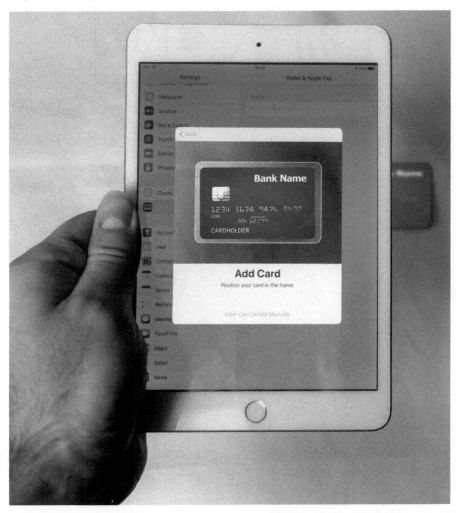

If you can't get the camera to scan the card, tap 'enter card details manually' then key in your card number, exp dates and so on.

Enter the security code from the back of your card. The bank will authorise your card. Accept the terms and conditions.

If you also have an iPhone, these cards will be synced with your iPhone so you can use Apple Pay on there too.

Using Apple Pay

You can use Apple Pay at any store that supports this feature. You will usually see the logo displayed in store. You can also use Apple Pay on some online stores.

To pay with Apple Pay, place your iPhone/iPad above the reader with your thumb on the home button without pressing it. You'll see a prompt on your iPhone for the amount - you authorise the payment using the finger print scanner on the home button.

If you want to pay with a card other than the default, hold the top of your iPhone near the contactless reader without touching the home button.

Tap the card you want to use.

Present your iPhone to the contactless reader with your thumb on the home button to complete payment.

Holding your thumb on the home button uses the finger print reader to verify your identity and is sometimes called 'touch id'.

Productivity Apps

Apple have developed three productivity apps that allow you to create documents and keynote presentations.

These apps don't usually come pre-installed, so you will need to download them from the app store.

You can do this by searching for 'essentials', then tapping on the 'get' icons for pages and keynote.

Creating Documents with Pages

To launch Pages, tap the icon on your home screen.

Once Pages 6 has opened, tap 'continue' on the welcome page. If you are launched Pages for the first time, you'll be asked to use iCloud. Click 'Use iCloud'. This enables you to save your documents to your personal cloud space. Next, tap 'create a document'.

You will now need to select a template.

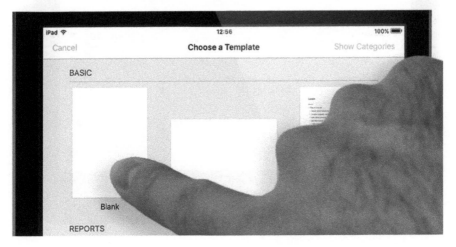

Chapter 6: Productivity Apps

Once you have selected the template to use you will see the main work screen. Let's take a closer look at the main editing screen.

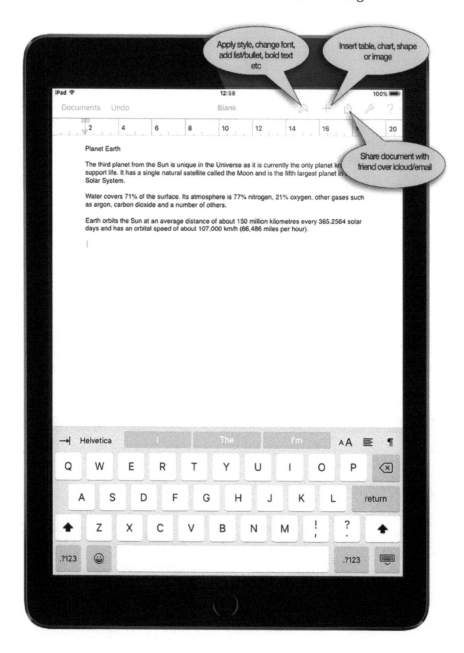

Formatting Text

Begin typing in your text into the main window as shown above.

The text we entered before needs formatting. To add a heading type it in above the block of text.

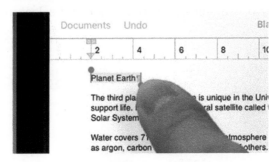

Highlight your text with your finger as shown above by dragging the blue dots over the text, then tap the paint brush from the toolbar.

Tap on 'title' to apple the title style to the selected text

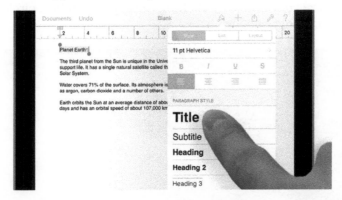

Formatting your document means laying it out in a style that is easy to read and looks attractive. This could involve changing fonts, making text bigger for headings, changing colour of text, adding graphics and photographs, etc.

For each document template you choose from the Template Chooser there are a number of pre-set paragraph styles. These are to help you format your document consistently, eg so all headings are the same font, size and colour.

Adding a Picture

The easiest way to add a picture is to tap the plus sign on the right hand side of the toolbar. Then from the dropdown, tap the image icon on the right. Select one of your albums if you want to insert a photo you took with your camera or tap 'insert from' if you have an image on your iCloud drive. Tap your pictures folder and select an image.

You can resize your image by clicking the resize handles, circled below, and dragging them.

support life. It has a single natural satellite called the Moon and is the fifth largest planet in the Solar System.

You can change the styles by adding borders and shadows by tapping on the paint brush icon on the top right of your toolbar.

196

Keynote

Keynote allows you to create multimedia presentations. To launch keynote, go to your home screen and tap keynote.

Tap continue, and if you're running keynote for the first time, tap 'use icloud'.

If you want to create a new presentation, tap 'new document' on the bottom left hand side of the window. From here you can select from a variety of pre-designed templates with different themes, fonts and colours.

Once you have selected a template you will see the main screen as shown below. This is where you can start building your presentation.

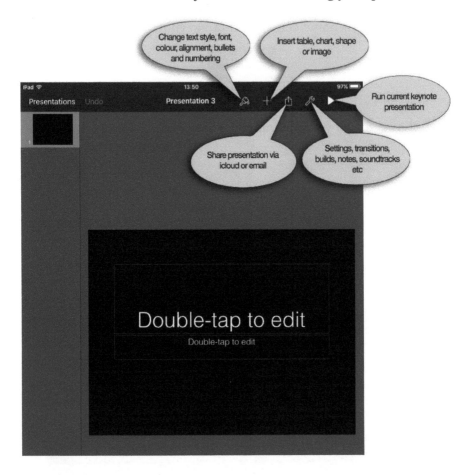

Editing a Slide

Double tap in the heading field shown above and enter a heading eg 'Planet Earth'. You can tap and drag the heading wherever you like.

Adding a New Slide

Tap the new slide button located on the bottom left of the screen, then tap a slide layout from the options that appear.

Add some text by double clicking on the text box that appears in the slide.

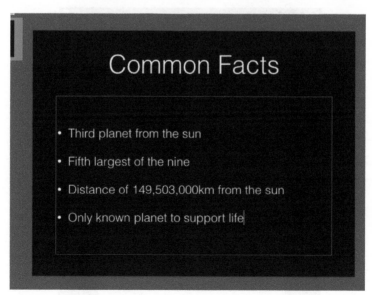

Adding Media

To add images and media to your slide, tap the plus sign on your tool bar at the top right of your screen. Then tap the image icon on the right.

If you want to add one of your photographs from your photo library, tap on one of your albums and select a photo. If you want to insert a picture from your iCloud, tap 'insert from...'

From your iCloud drive, select pictures. Tap on a picture.

Animations

Animations allow you to make objects such as text or photographs appear...

Tap on your text box and select the animate icon located on the top right corner of your screen

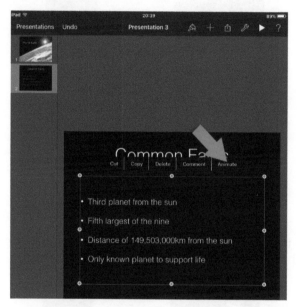

Then tap 'none: build in'

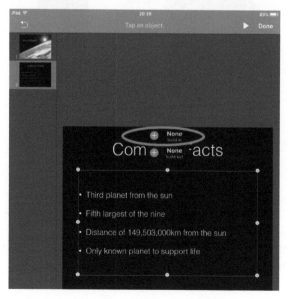

Then select an effect from the effects drop down menu (shown below).

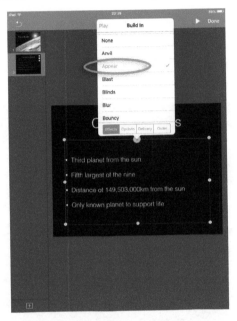

Then specify that you want the bullet points to appear one by one. Tap 'delivery' and select 'by bullet' from the drop down menu.

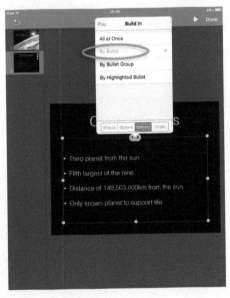

To see what the effect looks like, tap the play button on the top right of your screen.

Formatting Text Boxes

Tap on a text box you want to format. You can add borders to your text boxes, reflection effects or background colours.

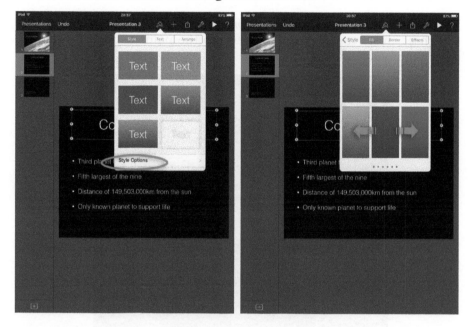

To format the border and fill your text box, tap your text box and tap the paint brush icon, on the top right of the screen.

Tap fill to change the background colour of the text box. Then swipe your finger across the selections of effects and tap on one to select it. In this example, I am going for a nice blue gradient fill.

Formatting Text Inside Textboxes

To change the formatting of the text, for example to change the colour of the text or make it bold.

First select your text in the text box you want to change. Tap on the text three times to select it all. Then tap the paint brush icon on the top right of your toolbar.

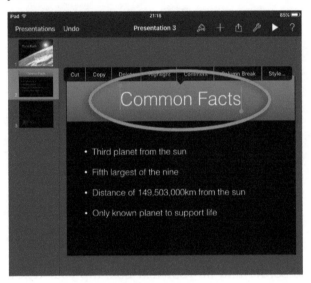

From here you can change the font, the font colour, size etc.

As an example I have changed the colour to light blue and made it bold.

Tap on the font name, illustrated with the red arrow. Then from here I can change the size, the colour and the typeface. You can change these by tapping on the icons down the right.

Other Apps

There are plenty of other productivity apps. Just go onto the app store, select the explore icon along the bottom, then tap productivity and scroll down the list. You can get Microsoft Office, writing and drawing tools, Google Docs and loads more.

Chapter 7

Maintaining Your iPad

The new iPads will ship with iOS 11, but if you need to update a previous model then you can do that here.

Apple has dropped support for iPad 2 and the iPhone 4s. iOS 11 will install on the following devices.

- iPad Pro models
- iPad Air models
- iPad 4th generation
- iPad mini 4
- iPad mini 3
- iPad mini 2

Before upgrading, make sure you have some time where you don't need to use your iPad as it will be temporarily inoperative while the installation takes place.

iPad Backups

You can backup your settings, apps and files to your iCloud account. Go to Settings, Tap on your account name, select 'iCloud', then sign in if you haven't already done so.

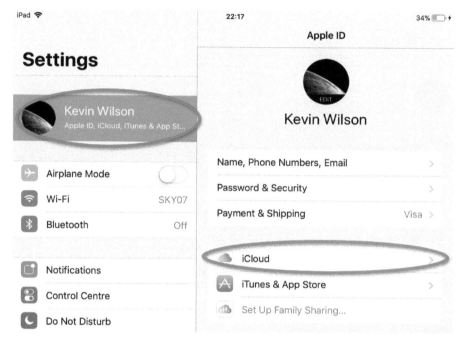

Tap 'Back Up Now'. This is usually the most common way.

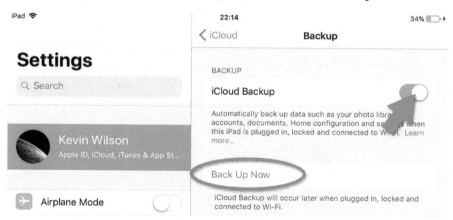

If you use iTunes, plug your device into your computer, select your iPad on the sidebar in iTunes, and select 'Back Up Now'. A backup will then be saved onto your computer's hard disk.

System Updates

To run the update, on your iPad open your settings app. Tap 'general' then select 'Software Update'.

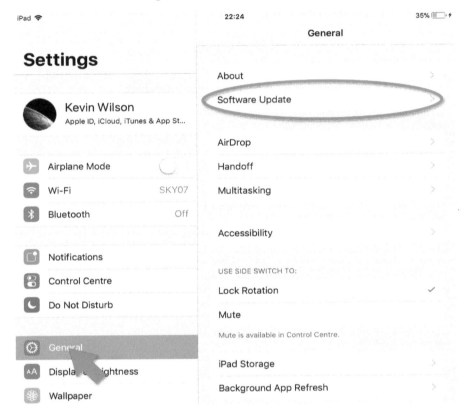

Make sure your device is connected to both Wi-Fi and a power supply, then tap Download and Install to do so.

Depending on your internet connection the installation might take a while.

208

If you prefer to update using iTunes. Connect your iPad using the cable to a USB port and select your device from the sidebar under devices.

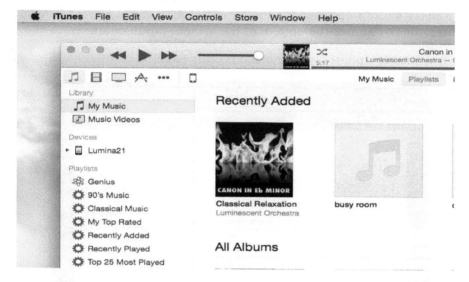

Under Summary, click 'Check for Update', then choose 'Download and Install'.

Confirm your iCloud details.

When updated, your iPad will restart automatically. You may have to run through the initial setup again outlined in chapter 1.

After this, your newly updated device should be ready to use.

App Updates

To check for app updates, tap the App Store icon on your home screen. From the bar across the bottom of the screen, tap updates.

Any available updates will be listed on this page.

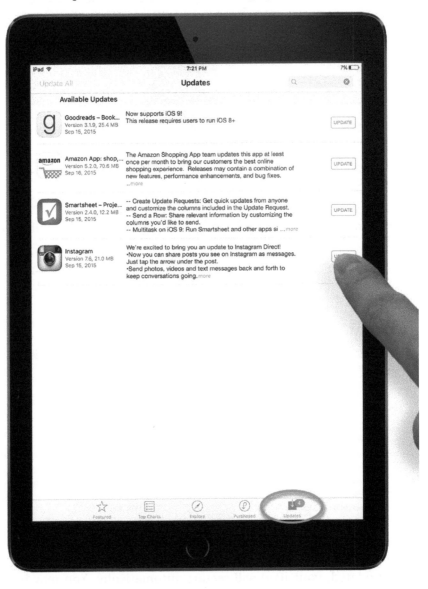

Tap 'update' to update that particular app.

Deleting Apps

To delete apps, tap and hold your finger on an app, until the X appears on the icon.

Tap on the X to delete the app.

Introduced in iOS 10, you can now delete any of the pre-installed apps, you don't use in the same way as above.

iPad Storage Maintenance

This gives you a view of the storage space available on your iPad with some features for freeing up storage space automatically. You can set your iPad to delete move your photos onto the iCloud photo library, empty your 'recently deleted' photos and albums, delete old conversations from iMessage, offload unused apps when your storage runs low and allows you to review large email attachments and messages and whether to keep them or move them off your iPad and onto iCloud.

Open your settings app, tap 'general', then select 'iPad storage'.

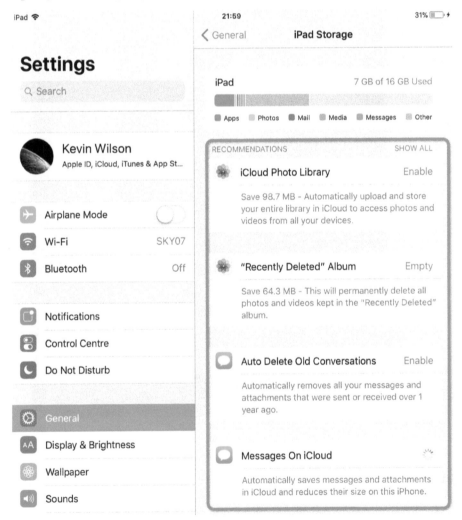

Tap on 'enable' to turn the feature on.

If you scroll further down the list, you'll see a list of individual apps that are currently installed on your iPad. Tap on an app to view details about storage.

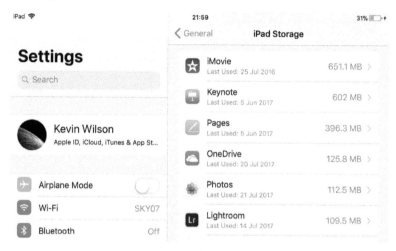

You can manually offload the app. Do this by tapping 'offload app'.

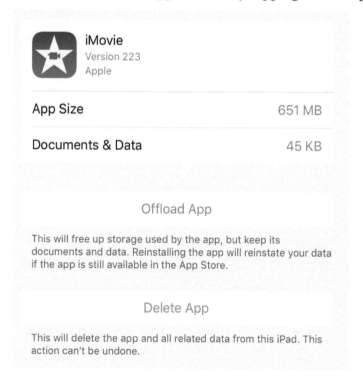

Or you can delete the app. Do this by tapping 'delete app'.

Chapter 8

Accessorise Your iPad

There are thousands of different accessories available for the iPad and you can buy them from a number of different manufacturers, not only Apple.

You just need to keep in mind the size and model of your iPad when shopping for accessories. Make sure it will fit the model you have; iPad mini, air, pro, etc.

Smart Keyboards

You can get USB and bluetooth keyboard from a variety of different manufacturers, not just Apple, and make a great little alternative to the on screen keyboard, when you are doing a lot of typing, writing or emailing.

Cases

A case is a must. You can get hundreds of different types. The ones I find most useful are ones that allow you to stand your iPad up making it great for watching movies. The case folds over covering the screen of the iPad when not in use.

USB Adapters

These come in useful when you want to connect something to your iPad and most peripherals, if they are not wireless, connect via USB.

These can be keyboards, mice, external hard drives, USB memory sticks, cameras, some models of printers and memory card readers.

AV Adapters

AV Adapters are useful if you want to connect your iPad to a TV, Monitor or Projector.

You can buy a small adapter that plugs into the port on the bottom of your iPad and will enable you to connect to an HDMI or DVI/VGA connector on your TV or Projector. Most modern TVs and Projectors are HDMI.

DVI

VGA

HDMI

Power Chargers

You can get a whole range of chargers from all different manufacturers. The most useful ones I have found are the ones that have a powered USB port on the side, that allows you to plug in your iPad and any other tablet for that matter, using the cable that came with.

Index

Index

G

H

I

K

L

M

Index